LO

CAREERS

VAULT GUIDE TO

LIBRARY CAREERS

LIBRARY CAREERS

VAULT GUIDE TO
LIBRARY CAREERS

BY DEBORAH SOMMER and the staff of vault

Library of Congress CIP Data is available.

ISBN 13 : 978-1-58131-619-3

ISBN 10 : 1-58131-619-4

Printed in the United States of America

ACKNOWLEDGMENTS

Deborah Sommer's acknowledgments: Thank you to my colleagues who were so generous with their time, thanks to my family and friends for their wonderful support and thanks to the great people at Vault—especially Matt Thornton for his patience.

Vault's acknowledgments: We are extremely grateful to Vault's entire staff for all their help in the editorial, production and marketing processes. Vault also would like to acknowledge the support of our investors, clients, employees, family and friends. Thank you!

Table of Contents

Visit Vault at **www.vault.com** for insider company profiles, expert advice,
career message boards, expert resume reviews, the Vault Job Board and more.

V/\ULT CAREER LIBRARY   viii

Visit Vault at **www.vault.com** for insider company profiles, expert advice,
career message boards, expert resume reviews, the Vault Job Board and more.

VAULT CAREER LIBRARY

ix

ON THE JOB   107

Chapter 7: Career Paths and Lifestyle   109

Chapter 8: Librarian Profiles   125

FINAL ANALYSIS   137

APPENDIX   141

Helpful Resources   143

Visit Vault at **www.vault.com** for insider company profiles, expert advice,
career message boards, expert resume reviews, the Vault Job Board and more.

VAULT CAREER LIBRARY

x

ABOUT THE AUTHOR   151

Visit Vault at **www.vault.com** for insider company profiles, expert advice,
career message boards, expert resume reviews, the Vault Job Board and more.

V/AULT CAREER LIBRARY   xi

INTRODUCTION

Introduction

Superhero or Spinster?

Barbara Gordon was a librarian by day but spent her nights as the superhero Batgirl. She went on to serve in the U.S. House of Representatives, hanging up her bat wings briefly. After her stint as a Congresswoman she returned to Gotham City and resumed her role as Batgirl until she became paralyzed after being shot by The Joker. So what did Babs do? She fell back on her super intellect, her expert knowledge of computers, experience as a hacker and her training as a librarian. Barbara became known as Oracle, and continued working as a modern day librarian/information broker—searching for information and gathering intelligence to assist law-enforcement agencies and, of course, her fellow superhero crime fighting community. Of course, Barbara (a/k/a Batgirl and Oracle) only lived in DC Comics and later in books, but what a role model!

Jet Li played a librarian in the movie *Black Mask*; Katharine Hepburn showed Spencer Tracy the right way to do research in *Desk Set*, and the sultry librarian and martial arts expert Evelyn (played by Rachel Weisz) is no shrinking violet in the remake of *The Mummy*. One of the more popular characters in popular culture today is the endearingly geeky Yomiko Readman, a bibliophile who works as an agent for the British Library's Special Operations Division. In *Operation Document Retrieval*, Yokimo fights to recover manuscripts stolen from the Library of Congress (after its destruction). Yomiko was first introduced in a series of novels (nine at this writing) set in a fictional universe known as R.O.D. or Read or Die, and her popularity continues in Japanese anime and manga, television spin-offs, fan websites, and merchandise including T-shirts, trading cards and a figurine of Yomiko (which sells for about $150). If it weren't for Rupert Giles, the school librarian who doubles as "The Watcher" in *Buffy and the Vampire Slayer*—poor Buffy might have been history quite early in the WB television series.

On the flip side of the coin, there are more than enough portrayals in the past and today that stereotype the librarian as a grumpy (and frumpy) silencing character, usually with her hair in a bun, her finger raised to her lips, peering over her glasses and a stern look on her face. From *The Rugrats* to Irma Pince in the Hogwarts library of the *Harry Potter* novels, librarians are just as often shown in a negative light. Every holiday season when *It's a Wonderful Life* can be found on television around the clock, viewers are reminded what a horrific life Donna Reed would have had as a librarian had George Bailey (James Stewart) not heeded his guardian angel's warnings. Furthermore, *Star Wars Episode II: The Attack of the Clones* gives us crotchety librarian Jocasta Nu, Nick-at-Nite's *All That* has The Loud Librarian who scolds anyone for the slightest noise, even a cough; and finally, Noah Wyle should stick to ER because he was quite a wimp in the made-for-TV movie *The Librarian*.

Above all, information-keepers

So, are librarians superheroes, individuals with photographic memories and vast storage random access brains? Or are they the stern looking women (or men) who guard the books, keep unruly library users under control and constantly tell people to be quiet with either a shush or a look?

Most librarians and those who work with them would probably settle on something in between. All types of individuals are found in the profession of librarianship and working in paraprofessional or clerk positions in libraries. It's not so much about the books these days as it is about information regardless of the format: print, electronic or digital. As for gloom and doom predictions of the demise of libraries and the superfluity of librarians, many predict that ongoing technological innovations will only continue to create better access and organization of information to serve users. Who will be behind these innovations? Librarians, of course.

CAREERS

THE SCOOP

LIBRARY

CAREERS

The History of Libraries

CHAPTER 1

Early Origins

The word library probably originates from liber, the Latin word, and the Greek word bibliotheke. In Latin, bibliotheca means a collection of books or library. As for libraries themselves, an ongoing debate continues about their origins. Archeological digs in Sumer, an ancient civilization (around 6000 BC) located in the southern part of Mesopotamia (modern day southeastern Iraq), discovered hundreds of thousands of texts in the Sumerian language—the great majority of these on clay tablets. These Sumerian texts included personal and business letters and transactions, receipts, lexical lists, laws, hymns and prayers, magical incantations and scientific texts, including mathematics, astronomy, and medicine.

The first librarian

The first librarian is thought to have been Amit Anu of the Royal Library of Ur in one of the major cities of Sumer (2000 BC), who held the title "Tabl Keeper." Other early librarians were those at the great library of Alexandria—Zenodotus of Ephesus, holding that post until 245 B.C.E. His successor, Callimachus of Cyrene, was Alexandria's most famous librarian, creating for the first time a subject catalog in 120,000 scrolls of the library's holdings, called the Pinakes, or Tables.

The first public library

The library of Alexandria is frequently considered the first public library, though there did exist numerous private libraries in earlier times. The libraries of the Roman Empire were probably the first to be open to the public. These libraries were collections of scrolls, which were available for viewing but were not allowed outside of the library. When the Roman Empire fell and later in 1400 AD, when the libraries of Constantinople were also destroyed, many of the scrolls and books were burnt as fuel.

In the ninth century in Northern Africa and the Middle East there were libraries called "halls of science" which were run by Islamic sects. These libraries were open to the public, but, again, few offered lending privileges.

The First American Academic Library

In the United States, one of the first major moments for the library occurred at Harvard; the university's library, founded in 1638 with the bequest of 400 books from John Harvard, was the first academic library in America. Today, Harvard has over 90 libraries with over 16 million books, making it the largest academic library in the world and putting it in a distinct category with other great libraries, including The Library of Congress (described below), The British Library, The New York Public Library and the Bibliothèque Nationale de France.

The Library of Congress

The establishment of the Library of Congress was another significant step in American library history. It was brought into being in 1800 by an act of Congress under President John Adams. The legislation originally was intended to set up a research library for the use of Congress providing "such books as may be necessary for the use of Congress—and for putting up a suitable apartment for containing them therein ..." The original library was housed in the Capitol until 1814, when British troops set fire to the building and destroyed the library.

Former President Thomas Jefferson donated his personal library, at the time considered the finest in the United States. His collection included books in foreign languages and volumes of philosophy, science, literature and other topics perhaps not relevant to congressional research. He wrote, "I do not know that it contains any branch of science which Congress would wish to exclude from their collection; there is, in fact, no subject to which a Member of Congress may not have occasion to refer."

A continuing mission

The Jeffersonian belief that all subjects are important to the library of the American legislature is the philosophy and rationale behind the comprehensive collecting policies of today's Library of Congress.

A new building housing the Library of Congress opened its doors to the public on November 1, 1897. Today the Library of Congress is the largest in the world, with more than 130 million items on approximately 530 miles of bookshelves. The collections include more than 29 million books and other printed materials, 2.7 million recordings, 12 million photographs, 4.8 million maps and 58 million manuscripts.

To continue the original mission of the Library of Congress, Congress created the Legislative Reference Service in 1914, which was renamed the Congressional Research Service in 1970. Its mission is to provide Congress with comprehensive and reliable analysis, timely, confidential, objective and nonpartisan research and information services.

And the library's influence extends beyond Congress. Larger libraries, usually larger colleges, universities and research institutions, adopted The Library of Congress Classification System, which allows for much more specificity of subject classification and organization.

Early Library Education

The father of librarianship

Melvil Dewey is considered the "father" of modern librarianship. In 1887 he started the first program to educate librarians at Columbia University. Despite the existence of many libraries in the United States and throughout the world, these libraries were not run or staffed by professionally schooled or trained librarians. In stating the mission of this first school, Dewey said "There is already an overstock of mediocre librarians, assistants and catalogers, and the influence of the school is intended to diminish rather than increase their numbers."

Dewey is also known for the Dewey Decimal System, a letter and numbering system still in use in smaller, primarily public libraries to classify and organize their books.

Dewey's program

The first class at Columbia was made up of 20 students who undertook a four-month course, which later became a two-year program as was typical at the time for law and medical schools. The curriculum was made up of courses that included languages and comparative literature, as well as the advanced work in bibliography, cataloging, classification and of topics related to library management, then known as library economy.

The technology of the day was the pen and the hand. One of the important skills taught in those early days was something called the "library hand," a

Visit Vault at www.vault.com for insider company profiles, expert advice, career message boards, expert resume reviews, the Vault Job Board and more.

VAULT CAREER LIBRARY

9

very fine and precise handwriting that allowed students and, later, librarians to properly pen catalog records or cards. In fact, applicants to the library school were asked to submit handwriting samples to be evaluated and critiqued for further development. Bibliography was then considered anything that increased the knowledge of books. The general education component of the program was primarily languages—the most important were German, French, and Latin, not as philosophy but as working tools.

The rest of the program and training involved visiting libraries to see the methods of work, catalogs, and visits to binderies, printing offices and bookstores.

In a report published in 1887 in *Library Notes*, Dewey described the beginning of this first professional program, or library school, and stated, "Evidently the time is not far distant when a man or woman seeking the place of a librarian without training for its duties will be thought as much a quack or charlatan as the physician seeking patients without having attended a medical school or served an apprenticeship with an accomplished practitioner.

A growing field

Dewey was on to something, even though it didn't happen overnight. Prior to the middle of the 20th century, library education was traditionally taught by academic librarians in conjunction with colleges of education. In the late 1940s, library education nationwide saw the development of library schools that had their own teaching faculty and were not always part of colleges of education but became separate schools within universities.

Monumental moments in early U.S. library history

1638 – First academic library was founded at Harvard University.

1731 – First "social" library was founded by Benjamin Franklin.

1748 – Charleston Library Society was founded.

1800 – Library of Congress established.

1849 – New Hampshire was the first state to pass a law to allow taxes to support libraries.

1854 – The Boston Public Library, the first publicly funded library, opened.

1876 – *Library Journal*, the oldest independent library publication in the United States, was founded.

1876 – Melvil Dewey published the Dewey Decimal System.

1876 – Melvil Dewey, Justin Winsor and William Frederick Poole were among the founders of the American Library Association in Philadelphia.

1876 – Charles Cutter wrote a statement on the status of cataloging in the United States and developed the standard for the dictionary catalog.

1887 – Melvil Dewey established the first Library School at Columbia University.

1890 – The first statewide organization of librarians, The New York Library Association was founded.

1892 – Landmark model legislation for development of school libraries in New York state was passed.

1896 – The National Education Association (NEA) created a Library Section.

1897 – Library of Congress was opened to the public.

1920 – The Carnegie Estate donated $50 million to build 2,500 libraries.

Visit Vault at www.vault.com for insider company profiles, expert advice,
career message boards, expert resume reviews, the Vault Job Board and more.

VAULT CAREER LIBRARY   11

Public Libraries

The genesis of the public library was actually a subscription or social library. Benjamin Franklin started a subscription library in 1731, which later became the Library Company of Philadelphia in 1742. Individuals could buy shares in the Library Company to join the "library." In 1748, the Charleston Library Society was founded in Charleston, South Carolina, and claims to be the third-oldest library in the United States. Unlike many early membership or subscription libraries, the Charleston Library Society is still open today to the public with varying membership fees.

In the 1800s, mercantile libraries were funded by the wealthy and aimed at the middle and lower classes. These libraries were typically owned by companies and used by their employees "to promote orderly and virtuous habits, diffuse knowledge and the desire for knowledge, improve the scientific skill and create good citizens."

Evolving definitions

In 1876, "public library" had a different meaning than our present definition. Most people today define "public library" as tax supported, open to all and administered by local government. In 1876 "public library" was more broadly defined and included any library open to any segment of the population. Therefore, an academic library in 1876 was, by that definition, a public library. The distinctions between type of library (school, public, academic and special) were less clear-cut than they aretoday.

Thank you, Mr. Carnegie

Public libraries, as we now know them, became widespread due to the largess of Andrew Carnegie. Over 2,500 public and university libraries were built with money donated by Carnegie between 1883 and 1929. The first of the Carnegie libraries in the United States was built in 1889 in Braddock, Pennsylvania, where one of the Carnegie steel mills was located. Almost all the towns that requested a Carnegie grant to build a library and agreed to Carnegie's terms were given the funds: The terms required that they demonstrate the need for a public library, provide the building site and then provide on an annual basis 10 percent of the original amount of the construction to support the library's operation.

In addition to putting libraries in small towns, the Carnegie libraries were the first to have open "stacks," which allowed library users to browse among the books and select what they wanted to read.

"There is not a cradle of democracy upon the earth as the Free Public Library, this republic of letters, where neither rank, office, nor wealth receives the slightest consideration." —Andrew Carnegie

School Libraries

The history of American school libraries can be traced to the public library movement in the last half of the 19th century. At that time, public libraries served the needs of public schools, which were often built in close proximity to a public library. Public library staff frequently placed temporary book collections in the schools for educators' use.

In the early part of the 20th century, educators became more aware of the importance of libraries. During this time, secondary schools continued to receive services from public libraries. Elementary schools had classroom collections, which became the core collection when school libraries were formed. In 1906, Virginia's first school library opened its doors, then in 1914 the American Library Association created the School Library section.

Post-war development

The period after World War II saw a growth in the development of school libraries, the development of technology and the application of technology in education. A new format film and its varying formats (filmstrip, slide, etc.), which had been used in military training, became accepted forms of instructional technology in schools.

On October 4, 1957 the Soviet Union launched the first earth satellite, Sputnik, into orbit, prompting the United States to step up its space program. Congress passed the National Defense Education Act (NDEA) in 1958 to train scientists and engineers, and to strengthen science, foreign language and mathematics instruction in the public schools. These initiatives led to a period of tremendous national growth in school library programs in the 1960s, bolstered by an influx of federal funding.

Foundation and federal support

In 1963, The Knapp Foundation of North Carolina funded the Knapp School Libraries Project (1963 to 1974). The American Library Association used funds provided by the Knapp Foundation to fund the School Library Manpower Project (1968 to 1974), which developed library job descriptions; and set up six model library science education programs

Visit Vault at **www.vault.com** for insider company profiles, expert advice, career message boards, expert resume reviews, the Vault Job Board and more.

V∧ULT CAREER LIBRARY   **13**

at Arizona State, Auburn, Mankato State, Millersville State, University of Denver and University of Michigan.

Continued federal support for school libraries increased funds to purchase library materials and equipment. Then, as part of Lyndon Johnson's War on Poverty, the Elementary and Secondary School Act Title I was passed, providing more funds to purchase library materials and textbooks.

Quality and freedom

In 1972, the Commonwealth of Virginia adopted the first Virginia Standards of Quality, which included the hiring of library professionals to staff school libraries.

There are few other countries in the world that have a free and open system of libraries similar to that in the United States. Even in those countries that do have research or academic libraries, researchers in many cases must make appointments to use the collections, and frequently are not allowed to browse freely in the book stacks or even check the books out.

"The library connects us with the insight and knowledge, painfully extracted from Nature, of the greatest minds that ever were, with the best teachers, drawn from the entire planet and from all our history, to instruct us without tiring, and to inspire us to make our own contribution to the collective knowledge of the human species. I think the health of our civilization, the depth of our awareness about the underpinnings of our culture and our concern for the future can all be tested by how well we support our libraries."—Carl Sagan, *The Cosmos*

Defining Librarianship

CHAPTER 2

What is a librarian?

According to the *Random House Unabridged Dictionary*, a librarian is "a person trained in library science and engaged in library service; a person in charge of a library, especially the chief administrative officer of a library, a person who is in charge of any specialized body of literature."

What is librarianship?

Librarianship is defined by the same source as "a profession concerned with acquiring and organizing collections of books and related materials in libraries and servicing readers and others with these resources."

These definitions, though accurate, are quite vague and tell little about librarians and the profession of librarianship.

Librarians Today

Librarians and libraries have changed drastically over the last 20 years. Instead of warehouses for books and other print resources, libraries are being redefined as information centers, learning centers or information commons. Libraries are now not so much places as they are sources and providers of information in any form to serve their users.

What librarians do

Librarians organize and provide access to information, whether it is print materials, such as books, magazines and journals, or CDs, DVDs, music scores, maps, electronic books (ebooks), electronic journals (ejournals), and numerous databases containing full-text articles or data. Libraries and librarians develop the technology to deliver much of this information to a user's desktop (or laptop) whether it be a student, a business person or a grandmother in rural Illinois looking for information to help her grandson with his history homework.

Bring on the technology

As a result, librarians (or, in current parlance, information professionals) increasingly are combining traditional duties with work involving technology. Librarians help and/or teach people to find information, show them how to evaluate it and use it effectively for academic, personal and professional purposes.

Goodbye, index cards

Where's the card catalog these days? Where else? Listed on eBay, where many find the antiquated cabinets to be collector's items. Recently a 24-drawer oak card catalog was listed with $799 in bids in the first few days of the auction.

On the 'Net

Librarians today are trained and educated in database searching, information management and information literacy. So all those users frustrated at the thousands of hits they get when they do a Google search should be turning to their librarians, who can teach users to be better Google searchers by evaluating the information they retrieve. The saying used to be "Just because you read it in a book or magazine doesn't necessarily make it true or accurate." The same sentiment goes double for websites. Students, young and old, don't always know which sources are reliable or blatantly false, propaganda or spoofs. Google searchers also find that commercially produced information is rarely available free online. So where do Google users turn when they are continuously asked to get out their credit cards to get the information they need? Again, they should look to their library and their librarians.

"Ask a librarian"

To wit, a good coupling of technology with old-fashioned reference and information service is the online "Ask a Librarian" services offered by many librarians. Some libraries only provide e-mail reference service, but many are now providing "real-time" service. These services are called virtual reference, providing 24/7 online access to a librarian and library resources. OCLC (Online Computer Library Company) offers a service to libraries that allows them to use 24/7 Questionpoint software, so librarians in their libraries and/or librarians contracted to be backup or after-hours librarians, are ready and willing to answer questions via internet chat around the clock. This is critical to the continued viability of libraries, since Generation Y (often referred to as the Netgens) and their subgroup, the younger iGeneration, have grown up with online chat or instant messaging (IM). The OCLC service used by many libraries, both public and academic, is typically renamed or branded by the home library or library system so it appears as a link on their webpage as California AskNow, Illinois AskAway, or other similar service allowing library patrons to "Ask a Librarian."

Librarians on Google

What do actual librarians make of Google's increasing influence? Some librarians worry that Google will take over their jobs, but others see the site as a great resource—particularly Google Scholar (www.scholar.google.com), which will link to a library's own resources. Even a novice Google searcher will turn up a considerable amount of information that has been written or produced by reliable sources—even by librarians.

Core Values of Librarianship

Librarians today rely on an important set of core values that help define, inform and guide their professional work. In addition to the core values below, librarians and the American Library Association (ALA) have developed policy statements of great importance, particularly today, related to the freedom to read, the Patriot Act and internet-related acts.

Free access to information

All information resources that are provided directly or indirectly by the library, regardless of technology, format or methods of delivery, should be readily, equally and equitably accessible to all library users.

Confidentiality/privacy

Protecting user privacy and confidentiality is necessary for intellectual freedom, and fundamental to the ethics and practice of librarianship.

Democracy

As Thomas Jefferson once said, "Information is the currency of democracy." A democracy presupposes an informed citizenry. The First Amendment mandates the right of all persons to free expression, and the

Visit Vault at **www.vault.com** for insider company profiles, expert advice, career message boards, expert resume reviews, the Vault Job Board and more.

VAULT CAREER LIBRARY

17

corollary right to receive the constitutionally protected expression of others. The publicly supported library provides free and equal access to information for all people of the community the library serves.

Diversity

Libraries and librarians value our nation's diversity and strive to reflect that diversity by providing a full spectrum of resources and services to the communities they serve.

Education and lifelong learning

ALA promotes the creation, maintenance and enhancement of a learning society, encouraging its members to work with educators, government officials and organizations in coalitions to initiate and support comprehensive efforts to ensure that school, public, academic and special libraries in every community cooperate to provide lifelong learning services to all.

Intellectual freedom

Libraries and librarians uphold the principles of intellectual freedom and resist all efforts to censor library resources.

The public good

ALA reaffirms the fundamental values of libraries in the context of discussing outsourcing and privatization of library services. These values include that libraries are an essential public good and are fundamental institutions in democratic societies.

Preservation

The association supports the preservation of information published in all media and formats. The association affirms that the preservation of information resources is central to libraries and librarianship.

Professionalism

The American Library Association supports the provision of library services by professionally qualified personnel who have been educated in graduate programs within institutions of higher education. It is of vital importance that there be professional education available to meet the social needs and goals of library services.

Service

Librarians provide the highest level of service to all library users. They strive for excellence in the profession by maintaining and enhancing their own knowledge and skills, by encouraging the professional development of co-workers, and by fostering the aspirations of potential members of the profession.

Social responsibility

ALA recognizes its broad social responsibilities. The broad social responsibilities of the American Library Association are defined in terms of the contribution that librarianship can make in ameliorating or solving the critical problems of society; support for efforts to help inform and educate the people of the United States on these problems and to encourage them to examine the many views on and the facts regarding each problem; and the willingness of ALA to take a position on current critical issues with the relationship to libraries and library service set forth in the position statement.

Note: The above core values were adopted June 29, 2004, by the ALA Council.

Code of Ethics

The American Library Association has developed and prescribed the ethical principles that guide the work of librarians and others working in libraries and the information profession.

Since libraries and librarians influence the selection, organization, preservation and dissemination of information, the need for ethical guidelines are paramount; and libraries have a special obligation to ensure the free flow of information and ideas to present and future generations.

Withstanding censorship

The principles of the below code of ethics are broad but provide a framework to guide libraries when conflicts in values arise. Articulating these principles is especially important since the values expressed in the code are constantly challenged. Individual communities may exert pressure to have certain books or materials removed from their libraries, in effect calling for censorship. Nationally, libraries have been in the news when defending their users' right to privacy by refusing federal law enforcement access to patron information—particularly what materials they have checked out or accessed.

The following codes were adopted by the American Library Association Council in 1995 at the ALA annual conference.

I.   We provide the highest level of service to all library users through appropriate and usefully organized resources; equitable service policies; equitable access; and accurate, unbiased and courteous responses to all requests.

II.   We uphold the principles of intellectual freedom and resist all efforts to censor library resources.

III.   We protect each library user's right to privacy and confidentiality with respect to information sought or received and resources consulted, borrowed, acquired or transmitted.

IV.   We recognize and respect intellectual property rights.

V.   We treat co-workers and other colleagues with respect, fairness and good faith, and advocate conditions of employment that safeguard the rights and welfare of all employees of our institutions.

VI.   We do not advance private interests at the expense of library users, colleagues or our employing institutions.

VII.   We distinguish between our personal convictions and professional duties, and do not allow our personal beliefs to interfere with fair representation of the aims of our institutions or the provision of access to their information resources.

VIII. We strive for excellence in the profession by maintaining and enhancing our own knowledge and skills, by encouraging the professional development of co-workers and by fostering the aspirations of potential members of the profession.

Where Librarians Work

CHAPTER 3

Librarians tend to be identified by the type of library in which they work. There are numerous types of libraries, including college, university or other academic library; corporate, government or other special library; school libraries; and public libraries. Some librarians work with specific groups, such as children, young adults or the disadvantaged. In school library media centers, librarians—often called school media specialists—help teachers develop curricula, acquire materials for classroom instruction, and assist and teach K-12 students on how to find information.

Colleges and Universities

When queried, a number of people, including college students, will say that they don't use their libraries. When you ask them how they do research for their class papers and projects, they'll say, "Oh, we have these really neat databases with full-text articles; and we can access them 24/7 from our dorm rooms." Those students may not know it but, yes, they are using their libraries. The librarians at their college or university have evaluated, purchased, organized and developed a webpage or research portal to make available the wide-array of databases and other electronic resources, including e-books, that students and faculty can access from their dorm rooms or offices.

College and university libraries are categorized by size. The Association of Research Libraries (ARL) is made up of 123 libraries at the largest and most prestigious research-oriented universities in the United States and Canada. Collectively this group of libraries spends over $1 billion a year on library resources.

Types of jobs

Jobs for librarians in academic libraries vary in their duties and often in the types of information, subject matter or audiences they work with. Johns Hopkins University Sheridan Library has librarians to work with their distance education programs to design and implement virtual library services to external organizations and institutions in secondary and higher education. Brown University Catalog/Metadata Librarian catalogs music and creates metadata for digital projects, and participates in evaluation and application of current and emerging metadata standards for multiple formats. Georgetown University Library has a Reference Librarian/Web Services Coordinator to support the teaching and research endeavors of the university community by providing reference services and coordinating the organization and content of the Georgetown University Library website. The Miami University Libraries, Oxford, Ohio, Life Sciences Librarian serves as liaison to the botany, microbiology and zoology departments in the College of Arts and Sciences, and is involved in reference service, collection development and library instruction. One of the many bibliographer/reference librarians at Vanderbilt University selects and manages collections to support graduate and undergraduate programs in English, Film Studies, and Theatre. Harvard University's Germanic Technical Services Department Head manages Germanic language acquisitions and cataloging operations. Temple University's Media Services Librarian selects audio, video, and digital media and media reference works, evaluates and implements new and emerging multimedia technologies and delivers user services including media editing assistance, media reference and instruction. And the diverse range of subjects and responsibilities goes on and on.

Employment numbers

In addition to the ARL academic libraries, there are over 3,500 college, community college and other university libraries in the United States. Academic libraries currently employ over 25,000 librarians and 70,000 support staff.

Public Libraries

The public library is an organization that is publicly supported by taxes or fundraising, and typically provides access to materials and services designed for the population it serves; it is open to anyone who is a citizen within its jurisdiction. Librarians and other personnel who work in public libraries are typically city, county or state employees. There are approximately 9,000 public libraries in the United States today and many of those have both a main location and branch libraries, which together place the total number public libraries closer to 18,000. Public libraries range in size from a very small library in a small town that may serve a community of less than 10,000 citizens, to large systems of libraries statewide, to large municipal libraries, such as the New York or Chicago Public Library.

Collections, services and programs

Collections, services and programs may differ from public library to public library since each is designed to serve its particular community. Typical public library collections will include books on the bestseller lists, popular fiction, large print materials, magazines, books on tape, and other audio and video collections. Public libraries are also more likely to have extensive genealogy and local history collections than other types of libraries.

Services offered by public libraries include reading programs for adults, young adults and children; book clubs, story hours, book talks, computer training, small business counseling, consumer health information, book delivery, bookmobile services and public community meeting rooms or auditoriums.

Types of jobs

The adult services manager at the Live Oak Public Libraries, Savannah, Georgia, is responsible for hiring, training and evaluating adult services personnel and the management of the adult collection including genealogy and business resources. The youth services librarian at the Haywood County Public Library in Waynesville, North Carolina, plans, publicizes, prepares and carries out library services for young people. The librarian supervises story times, seasonal programs for children and their families, summer reading club programming and events, book talks, visits to area elementary schools and library tours for school groups.

Employment numbers

Public libraries employ over 45,000 librarians and approximately 90,000 other paid staff. Public libraries typically have a board of directors made up of members of the community, and "Friends of the Library," groups which assist with fund raising and volunteer programs.

School Libraries

School libraries are part of a school or a school system that serves students from kindergarten through grade 12 (K-12). Many school libraries are called media centers or learning resource centers. School librarians may be

Visit Vault at **www.vault.com** for insider company profiles, expert advice, career message boards, expert resume reviews, the Vault Job Board and more.

VAULT CAREER LIBRARY   23

called library media specialists, media librarians or teacher librarians. School librarians collaborate with teachers to enhance students' education by teaching information research skills, selecting books, databases and multimedia resources to support the curriculum, and developing information literacy programs.

School libraries and librarians have a unique opportunity to teach students at any age effective use of information and how to evaluate information. Whether librarians are teaching students how to find books, magazines articles or information on the internet, they are teaching valuable information literacy skills that transcend the classroom and contribute to lifelong learning. Harold Howe, the U.S. Commissioner of Education under Lyndon Johnson, said, "What a school thinks about its library is a measure of what it thinks about education."

Types of jobs

The school librarian at the Potomac School in Virginia works to expand and promote the services and programs of the library, and is responsible for the acquisition and maintenance of audiovisual materials and equipment, promotion of AV collection to teachers and students, reference services, supervision of the library during school hours, and collaboration with other librarians and teachers on designing lessons and projects. The librarian of the town of Mansfield (CT) and Mansfield Public Schools develops and present programs for children from preschool through eighth grade in both school and public library settings.

Employment numbers

School librarians make up approximately 71,000 of the librarians employed in the United States, and almost another 100,000 non-librarians are employed in school libraries.

Special Libraries

Librarians also work in information centers or libraries in corporations and law firms; medical research centers and hospitals; news organizations, such as newspapers, television networks and online news services; government agencies and numerous other organizations that need specialized information to fulfill their mission.

These information professionals, or special librarians, play a unique role in gathering, organizing and coordinating access to the best available information sources for their parent organization, and contribute to turning that information into usable and sometimes profitable knowledge.

The full spectrum

For example, a special librarian working for a corporation might provide the marketing and sales department with information on competitors and potential clients, or provide the research and development division with information on trends, new processes and technical developments related to the company's products and industry. Starbucks has a librarian who specializes in competitive intelligence and concentrates on managing creative sourcing strategies, researching and analyzing market trends, and creating and maintaining a talent database. The Mercer Human Resource Management consulting firm, which employs over 13,000 staff worldwide, has a librarian who holds a "Knowledge Manager" position. This person is responsible for managing self-service tools that support enterprise proposal development processes, and also collaborates with proposal strategists and consultants to design and develop web sites, language databases, templates and online databases.

AARP employs a librarian as a senior research information specialist to assess business and information needs for developing ongoing consulting relationships with select groups of staff, departments and/or teams, as well as to design, deliver and promote value-added information services and products. In the health care field, the nonprofit Memorial Sloan-Kettering Cancer Center employs reference librarians/informationists to provide customer-oriented services for answering research and information questions, customized teaching and on-the-spot training. This person also conducts bibliographic searches as required by researchers, clinicians, health care professionals and support staff, and maintains ongoing search alerts based on clients' requirements.

Government positions

Government librarians work in over 1,200 libraries for state and federal government agencies. Some of the largest government libraries in the U.S. are the Library of Congress, the National Archives, the National Library of Education, the National Library of Medicine and the National Agricultural Library. The Federal Reserve Bank has a library manager responsible for managing all aspects of library operations, including the management of

Visit Vault at www.vault.com for insider company profiles, expert advice, career message boards, expert resume reviews, the Vault Job Board and more.

VAULT CAREER LIBRARY   25

library staff, the planning, budgeting and delivery of programs, services and resources specifically designed to meet the information needs of the bank, and to support public information programs.

The Smithsonian Institute employs a number of librarians, including a head of the special collections to oversee one of the nation's great rare book and manuscript collections. This librarian manages the Dibner Library of the History of Science and Technology and the Joseph F. Cullman 3rd Library of Natural History.

In addition to government libraries that serve specific agencies or focus on specific subjects, there are also over 300 military libraries that serve the armed forces and their families in the U.S. and overseas.

Employment numbers

The larger corporate and government libraries may employ from 10 to over 200 librarians, while the majority of special libraries employ only one librarian. Corporate and government libraries are the largest special librarian employers, but organizations as varied as museums, such as The Country Music Hall of Fame and The Art Institute of Chicago, also employ librarians who specialize in music and art history respectively. Even Celebrity Cruise Lines hires librarians to work on their cruise ships for six-month stints helping people find leisure reading, get their e-mail, monitor their investments and plan their port activities.

Approximately 9,600 special libraries or other organizations in the United States employ over 17,000 librarians.

Fee-based Information Centers and Non-Library Jobs

Librarians also work as consultants specializing in human resources, staff development and training; library facility design; strategic planning and needs assessments; communications, public relations and marketing; and preservation, digitization and database development.

Companies producing and selling services and products to libraries hire librarians as marketing representatives, trainers, product developers and customer service representatives. Many of the databases that libraries purchase or license are developed by librarians or other information professionals. Companies providing services such as book or periodical jobbers frequently hire librarians with experience working in acquisitions or a related area within an academic or public library. For example, EBSCO, an international corporation serving libraries and academic institutions, hires librarians as account service managers to educate its clients and prospective clients about its print and electronic products and services, and maintaining customer relationships by personal visits to academic, corporate, school and public libraries.

Search firms and employment agencies

Library placement services, executive search firms and temporary agencies also employ librarians to serve as career advisors, placement coordinators, researchers and head hunters. Library temporary agencies recruit librarians who wish to work part-time or in temporary jobs, and place them with libraries, organizations or companies that have short-term staffing needs or need librarians to manage or work on special projects.

For entrepreneurs

Entrepreneurial librarians may start up their own consulting firms, employment agencies or information services companies. Fee-based information services or information brokers provide research services, delivery of documents and reports, and other library-related services to clients on a project by project basis or provide services upon request to clients for an annual fee. Librarians who own or work in these companies provide information services to organizations of all sizes. In addition to research and information delivery, many of these information brokers also analyze the information and provide customized reports to assist their clients with operations or decisions within their business or other organization.

Similar in some extent to consultants and entrepreneurial librarians are librarians who work as independent contractors. Librarian independent contractors may do research and write content for online, fee-based libraries or websites; provide ongoing or short-term indexing, abstracting or cataloging services; or work for companies that provide after-hours online reference services.

Visit Vault at www.vault.com for insider company profiles, expert advice, career message boards, expert resume reviews, the Vault Job Board and more.

VAULT CAREER LIBRARY   27

Places you might be surprised to find a librarian

- MTV

- Your hospital room on rounds with doctors and medical students at a teaching hospital

- The Rock 'n' Roll Hall of Fame

- The other side of an online chat at 4 a.m.

- An advertising agency

- On your cruise in the ship's library

- CNN

- The Art Institute of Chicago

- The Baseball Hall of Fame

- *The Washington Post*

- The Monterey Bay Aquarium Research Institute

Where Do Libraries and Librarians Fit in an Organization?

Academic libraries

College and university libraries may be separate entities within a university with a dean or they may report to a vice president, chancellor or provost of academic affairs. The libraries also may be dispersed throughout the university and be located and funded by individual schools and college. For example, the school of law or the college of education may fund its own library at a university. At some academic institutions, librarians hold faculty status and rank, while at others they may be considered professional staff. At public colleges and universities, the librarians may also be considered state employees.

Public libraries

A public library typically falls within some agency of the city, county or state that provides its funding and whose citizens it serves. Librarians who work for public libraries are city, county or state employees.

School libraries

School libraries are a department within the school or school system they serve. School librarians may also be teachers and they are employees of the school or, in some cases, the city or the county. Private schools' librarians are employees of the school.

Special and corporate libraries

Corporate libraries or information centers may be a department within the corporate headquarters or a corporate location, or they may be part of a division of the corporation, such as the research and development division. In another scenario, a librarian or information professional could be embedded within teams in an organization and assigned to acquire and provide information related to the mission of the team. For example, within many large consulting firms like McKinsey & Company, librarians specialize in particular subjects and market areas, such as the forest products market or a consumer group like "active seniors," and provide consultants with requested information as well as ongoing information related to their teams' work.

Law firms, government agencies, hospitals, newspapers and news organizations, scientific foundations, museums and others primarily organize and provide information to support the mission of their parent organization.

Visit Vault at www.vault.com for insider company profiles, expert advice, career message boards, expert resume reviews, the Vault Job Board and more.

VAULT CAREER LIBRARY   29

CAREERS

GETTING HIRED

LIBRARY
CAREERS

Education

CHAPTER 4

Most librarians do not get their undergraduate degree in library science. There are undergraduate programs out there—but entry into the profession requires a minimum of an ALA (American Library Association) accredited master's in library and information science. There are a few occasions where equivalent experience is accepted, but those are rare.

Pre-Master's Experience

Many people work as student assistants in a library while in college or work in libraries in a nonprofessional position before deciding that they want to become a librarian. Working at a university or in an academic library that also has a library school (ALA accredited MLIS program) sometimes qualifies one for tuition remission—a good way to pay your way through school. Previous library work experience isn't necessary for entry-level jobs but it definitely gives one an edge in the job market. Even if you worked in a library as a student in college or as a volunteer at your public library, that is valuable experience and shows that you have some sense of what working in the profession will be like.

Undergraduate study

What type of undergraduate degree should you get or have to be a librarian? That's a big question and nobody has one answer. The majority of students are already in the midst of their undergraduate studies when they consider graduate school in library and information science, or they have already graduated, so a degree in any field is mostly prerequisite for the master's program. Liberal arts majors will always find a place as librarians but some more highly sought-after undergraduate degrees are business, any field in the sciences—biology, chemistry, health sciences and any degree related to computer science and technology. It is natural that those with business, chemistry, engineering, art and education degrees would gravitate toward librarian positions in those areas.

Librarianship and Information Degree Programs

There are over 50 American Library Association accredited graduate programs in library and information studies in the United States and Canada. The name for the master's degree for librarians can vary from university to university. Traditionally, the degree was called an MLS (master's in library science) but you will also find the degree called master's of library and information studies (MLIS), MA in librarianship, MS in librarianship, and, occasionally, a master's in education and library science.

Schools with programs accredited by the American Library Association

University of Alabama	www.slis.ua.edu
State University of New York – Albany	www.albany.edu/dis/
University of Alberta	www.slis.ualberta.ca
University of Arizona	www.sir.arizona.edu
University of British Columbia	www.slais.ubc.ca
State University of New York – Buffalo	informatics.buffalo.edu
University of California, Los Angeles	www.is.gseis.ucla.edu
Catholic University of America	slis.cua.edu
Clarion University of Pennsylvania	www.clarion.edu/libsci
Dalhousie University	sim.management.dal.ca
University of Denver	www.du.edu/LIS
Dominican University	www.gslis.dom.edu
Drexel University	www.cis.drexel.edu
Emporia State University	slim.emporia.edu
Florida State University	www.lis.fsu.edu
University of Hawaii	www.hawaii.edu/slis
University of Illinois	alexia.lis.uiuc.edu
Indiana University	www.slis.indiana.edu

University of Iowa	www.uiowa.edu/~libsci
Kent State University	www.slis.kent.edu
University of Kentucky	www.uky.edu/CIS/SLIS
Long Island University	www.cwpost.liu.edu/cwis/cwp/cics/palmer
Louisiana State University	slis.lsu.edu
McGill University	www.gslis.mcgill.ca
University of Maryland	www.clis.umd.edu
University of Michigan	www.si.umich.edu
University of Missouri-Columbia	sislt.missouri.edu
University of Montreal	www.ebsi.umontreal.ca
University of North Carolina-Chapel Hill	sils.unc.edu/index.htm
University of North Carolina–Greensboro (Conditional)	lis.uncg.edu
North Carolina Central University	www.nccuslis.org
University of North Texas	www.unt.edu/slis
University of Oklahoma*	www.ou.edu/cas/slis
University of Pittsburg	www.sis.pitt.edu
Pratt Institute	www.pratt.edu/sils
University of Puerto Rico	egcti.upr.edu
Queens College, City University of New York	qcpages.qc.cuny.edu/GSLIS
University of Rhode Island	www.uri.edu/artsci/lsc
Rutgers University	www.scils.rutgers.edu
St. John's University	new.stjohns.edu/academics/graduate/liberalarts/departments/library
San Jose State University	slisweb.sjsu.edu
Simmons College	www.simmons.edu/gslis
University of South Carolina*	www.libsci.sc.edu
University of South Florida*	www.cas.usf.edu/lis

Visit Vault at **www.vault.com** for insider company profiles, expert advice, career message boards, expert resume reviews, the Vault Job Board and more.

VAULT CAREER LIBRARY

35

Southern Connecticut State University*

www.southernct.edu/departments/ils

University of Southern Mississippi,   www.usm.edu/slis

Syracuse University*   http://www.ist.syr.edu

University of Tennessee*   www.sis.utk.edu

University of Texas - Austin   www.ischool.utexas.edu

Texas Woman's University (Conditional)*   www.twu.edu/cope/slis

University of Toronto   www.fis.utoronto.ca/index.htm

University of Washington*   www.ischool.washington.edu

Wayne State University   www.lisp.wayne.edu

University of Western Ontario   www.fims.uwo.ca

University of Wisconsin–Madison   www.slis.wisc.edu

University of Wisconsin–Milwaukee*   www.uwm.edu/Dept/SOIS

*also has distance education program

The American Library Association publishes the most up-to-date listings and details of universities offering accredited degrees. Its *Directory of Institutions Offering ALA-Accredited Master's Programs in Library and Information Studies* can be found at www.ala.org/ala/accreditation/lisdirb/lisdirectory.htm.

Judging programs

Schools will have names that range from the more traditional school of library and information science to the University of Washington's information school (I-School for short). Look at the curriculum for different types of schools. If you already have some idea of the career path you'd like to take and it requires some of the more traditional courses, like reference, cataloging, collection development, etc., you will want to know that the school you choose doesn't focus more heavily on technology. But even if you're going in a more traditional direction, you will still need to take courses in the technology area—like internet technologies and resources, design of information systems, and knowledge management. If you're unsure of what area of librarianship you want to go into, choose a school that offers the broadest spectrum of courses—everything from storytelling to intellectual freedom in libraries, to network system administration. In addition to looking at the program and course descriptions, you should look at the annual *U.S. News America's Best Graduate Schools* for details on the program's ranking.

If you do know exactly what you want to do, it's critical to make sure that the program you choose offers classes in the area in your chosen area of focus. If you're interested in becoming a rare books librarian, you'll need to ascertain that the programs you are interested in will adequately prepare you in this area.

The student experience

I am in the school media specialist program. I received my bachelor's in secondary education, integrated social studies from Kent State University in Kent, Ohio, and decided to come to UTK-SIS to further my education. I work as a graduate assistant for undergraduate admissions at UT and I am a student worker for the law library on UT's campus. I hope to work in a middle or high school library after graduation.

I'm enjoying the program so much and learning new things every day. Of great importance to me are the web development and general technology advances in regard to information organization. I am really enjoying becoming independent in terms of website creation and know that the knowledge I gain from the program regarding all technologies will help me stay on the same level as my middle school or high school students in the future.

The other great thing about SIS is you get to take classes with so many diverse students. Students are of all ages, coming from quite varying backgrounds. The quest to organize information really unites us all. Because we can all interact using Centra, even if we're states away, I have always had a great classroom experience.

—Sarah Hilker, SIS Student, University of Tennessee-Knoxville

Core and specialty curricula

All ALA accredited programs have core courses to provide general preparation for librarianship. Schools also offer specialized tracks or

Visit Vault at www.vault.com for insider company profiles, expert advice, career message boards, expert resume reviews, the Vault Job Board and more.

VAULT CAREER LIBRARY

37

courses with concentrations in a specific area of library and information studies (for example, technology, school librarianship, art librarianship, health science librarianship, database design, or rare books and archives). You should investigate the available classes and discuss other options for gaining specialized education and experience through the availability of independent studies and internships.

School websites offer descriptions of their curriculum as well as degree tracks that focus on a particular specialization. For example, a program in general librarianship typically prepares students to work in information organizations, including libraries, archives, network services and agencies. A specialty in information architecture and technology focuses on developing and managing information technologies, including web-based resources and networks to better meet the information needs of users. Other specializations include programs addressing specific library types: public, academic or special librarianship. There are specializations in different subjects—law, business, rare books, science and technology, music and others, as well as specializations that focus on a subset of the population, such as children, teens or seniors.

The curriculum for each specialty will have some core courses in common but after that they will diverge into required courses for the specialty, along with electives.

A curriculum for general librarianship may look like this:

Eight courses or 24 credit hours from the following list of courses. The courses comprise a "recommended path" for those who want to pursue a general program of study in librarianship.

Assessing Information Needs *or* Information Needs of Adults

Design & Production of Network Multimedia

Website development and administration

Planning, Evaluation & Financial Management

Management of Information Collections

Information Needs of Children *or* Information Needs of Young Adults

Information Services

Cataloging & Classification

A program specializing in school librarianship may have a curriculum similar to the following:

Required:

- Library and Information Technologies (three hours)
- Collection Management (three hours)
- Children's Materials and Services (three hours)
- Young Adult Materials and Service (three hours)
- Advanced Literature and Literacy (three hours)

Suggested to fulfill 15-credit hour requirement:

- Internet Reference and Research (three hours)
- Storytelling (two hours)
- Booktalking (two hours)

Electives may be chosen from any subject area or specialization.

A program specializing in information management or library automation might include the following core courses:

The Life Cycle of Information (two credits)

Information Behavior (four credits)

Information Resources, Services and Collections (four credits)

Organization of Information and Resources (four credits)

Information in Social Context (four credits)

Instructional and Training Strategies for Information Professionals (three credits)

Research Methods (four credits)

Management of Information Organizations (four credits)

One four-credit information technology core course, which you can choose from a menu of options, such as information retrieval, XML, conceptual database design and network system administration. (four credits)

Visit Vault at **www.vault.com** for insider company profiles, expert advice, career message boards, expert resume reviews, the Vault Job Board and more.

VAULT CAREER LIBRARY

39

Electives include:

- Project Management
- Web Development
- Information Management
- Chief Information Officer
- Organizational Analysis
- Information Architecture
- Systems Analysis
- Database Management
- Information Systems
- Software Development
- Technology Management
- Competitive Intelligence Consulting
- Knowledge Management

Research required

Regardless of the specialty, do your research. Investigate the different specialties, read curriculum and course descriptions. Talk to librarians about the schools they attended, read the student newsletters online at the school websites, read librarian and library student blogs about their experiences. It's a tough decision, especially if you choose a school that will require you to move across the country.

Demographics

Students entering each year in MLIS programs range in age from students who have just completed their undergraduate degree through returning students in their 40s or older.

Getting younger?

Recently the profession is attracting more students in their 20s, though there is no hard demographic data yet to support this. One graduate school that collects demographic data on its students lists its 29-years-old-and-younger group as 34 percent of its MLS and PhD students currently enrolled. One popular theory is that younger librarians are attracted to the profession because of its melding with technology, although the persistent myth that librarianship is a "graying profession" may also be attracting younger candidates who perceive a huge surplus of jobs in the industry. (Published articles in both professional library publications and the mainstream news continue to hype the fact that 25 percent of librarians will be 65 and retiring by 2009 with another 53 percent reaching that age by 2019, even though many vacant positions may go to non-MLS graduates, and some librarians don't actually retire at 65. Additionally, many of the vacant positions may be for upper-level experienced librarians.) Still, *U.S. News & World Report* lists librarians among its top 30 careers for 2009; of course, among that list it also includes hair stylists and genetic counselors.

The current body of library students, regardless of age, is 80 percent female and 20 percent male. Minority students make up about 11 percent, while a growing number (currently 6 percent) are international students.

The Application Process

When applying to a school, in addition to your test scores, you will need your official transcripts from all universities attended, reference letters, possibly a personal essay and a current curriculum vitae or resume.

Admission requirements may vary from university to university. Usually a bachelor's degree is required and most schools accept a minimum GPA — typically a B average.

Graduate record exam and other tests

Most schools also require GRE test scores. You should check with the programs to which you are considering applying to see whether they accept alternate exams, such as the MAT (Miller Analogies Test). International students may also be required to take the TOEFL exam (Test of English as a Foreign Language). If you've been out of school for a while, an exam like the GRE can be quite daunting. But there are a number of resources to help. Check your local area for GRE-prep classes, see if your local library has study guides or purchase your own from a book store and definitely look at the GRE website for information about the exam (www.ets.org/gre).

Visit Vault at **www.vault.com** for insider company profiles, expert advice, career message boards, expert resume reviews, the Vault Job Board and more.

VAULT CAREER LIBRARY

41

References and essays

You may also be asked to have three or more references write letters of recommendation, and some programs require an essay or written statement of your educational and professional goals related to the program. Some programs also require an in-person interview for admission.

Furthering your candidacy

This author was interested in becoming a business librarian. The school she attended offered only one class in business resources and information, so she took the opportunity in each of her other classes to see if her projects or papers could be business-related. For example, in a collection development class she did a collections project on resources needed for a small business library; in her history of libraries class she wrote about the history of a library in a major corporation; and in a reference and instruction class she developed resources to teach students how to find information on companies. Those are only a few of the things she did to better focus her studies.

Before making your final decision, you may want to schedule a campus visit to meet with admissions and faculty in the school. Some schools accept online applications while others require paper applications. Check with the admissions office for the degree program to get specifics on applying.

Working While Going to School

Is it possible to work full time while pursuing a degree? Definitely, and one of the advances that has made that possible is the MLIS program that also offers a distance degree. Many of the courses are online courses or webcast lectures, and most programs require a week or two on campus as well as a practicum or internship. When these degrees first emerged, the library community was uncertain about how qualified these "distance" students would be. There are some exceptional distance programs—the University of Illinois at Champaign-Urbana is one—but like all graduate programs, the quality can vary and what each student gets from each program depends a lot on how much he puts into it. Particularly self-motivated students are well-suited to distance programs; those who are disciplined can also manage to hold down a full-time job. Distance programs are now widely accepted, and if they are accredited by the American Library Association the degrees are just as valuable as the more traditional degrees.

Distance education programs

If you are restricted both geographically and financially from moving to attend school, you have a choice of a number of programs that offer the MLIS through distance education.

There are several types of distance programs. Some include face-to-face (or in-person) courses held in other locations. Check to see if the schools you are considering offer classes in other cities throughout the state. The next type is primarily face-to-face with select courses offered online. Your next option is primarily online with some "in person" courses required. This option may require one or two weeks in the summer or one weekend or two on-campus rather than a semester-long "in person" course. Programs that can be offered to you anywhere may be programs that are completely online and web-based, or offered using satellite or other broadcast methods or a mixture of the two.

My distance education experience

I earned my master's in library science through the University of Illinois's superb distance education program, LEEP. Because of the way the program is structured, my experience was, if anything, more intense and immersive than it might have been if I'd been on campus. The program begins with a two-week "boot camp" that introduces library science and lets students get to know each other. For me, real bonds were formed during boot camp that have lasted through my school years and beyond. The remainder of the classes are held in real time unlike most distance-ed classes in other programs, which take place entirely asynchronously. (One session of each class per semester is conducted on campus.) An audio feed lets students hear the instructor, and they can ask questions and start discussions in a chat room at the same time. This format encourages participation, even from students who might not participate in a physical classroom. Discussion continues through the week between class sessions on message boards, in which participation is usually mandatory. The workload was heavy, and getting it all done while working a full-time job was a challenge, but I felt like I was getting as thorough a grounding in library science as I would have in an on-campus program. My one complaint was that there were not enough required courses; I managed to get my degree without ever taking a

Visit Vault at **www.vault.com** for insider company profiles, expert advice, career message boards, expert resume reviews, the Vault Job Board and more.

VAULT CAREER LIBRARY   43

reference class, and although reference wouldn't have been directly relevant to my current career, I still think it should be a requirement.

I now work as an experience architect specializing in taxonomy and classification, which my course work in LEEP prepared me for very well—both through traditional studies such as cataloging and through courses in nontraditional subjects, such as interface design and information architecture. Although I am not working in a library, I consider myself a librarian, and a LEEPer, for life.

—Amy Silvers

In a way, going to library school was, for me, a natural consequence of deciding that I wanted to make a career of working in libraries. It took me a long time to realize that I wanted to be a librarian—though I've always enjoyed using libraries, my post-college goal was to become a professor and teach at a college or university. During my postgraduate years, I ended up partially financing my education by working in a couple of academic libraries, including several "divisional libraries" in the Vanderbilt University library system; and as I became less enamored of the idea of becoming a full-time teacher (not to mention less engaged in my dissertation) and more intrigued by what librarians do—I was working for technical services at the time and getting an introduction to what one of my library school classes would call "the organization and representation of information"—I began to consider the notion of making a future in the library. A few years later, permanently ABD and in a public services library job, I decided to formalize the process, and enrolled in library school.

I ended up attending the School of Information Sciences at the University of Tennessee at Knoxville through its distance program. Why a distance program? Probably the most compelling reason was that I was working in a full-time job at the Peabody Library at Vanderbilt, and physically attending a program would have meant giving up that job (and the income associated with it), moving somewhere else for what was likely only to be a couple of years, and then, quite probably, having to move somewhere else after the program was finished to take another job—assuming I would be so fortunate to land something. (The fact that my wife would have to do all of this as well helped to cement the distance option in my mind.) Initially, I was a bit concerned about whether I would like attending classes by computer and not spending much time at all with my classmates and professors—I'd never done such a thing before. It actually turned out pretty well; the fact that I had already gotten more than one graduate degree via the traditional approach meant that I'd already had the experience of suffering together in the (physical) presence of fellow graduate students, and I didn't think it was necessary to have that experience again.

Of course, I was able to work face-to-face with some of my fellow students who also worked at Vanderbilt, and there were opportunities to connect up in "First Life" with others; but the amount of contact would still have been much less than being on site. Did I have any problems with the distance program? Probably my central criticism of the distance format is that distance students were not able to partake of the full range of courses that the on-site students had before them. While this makes sense in some situations—a course on preservation that requires hands-on work would be hard to do virtually—I'm not sure the rationale was always that clear. Overall, I'd have to say that the option of taking classes virtually was extremely beneficial for me in a number of ways, but I think each person who is considering such a move needs to think seriously whether it would be best for them in their particular context.

—*Chris Benda, Divinity Library, Vanderbilt University*

Internships and Practicums

Classes are the background and theory but the importance of internships and practicums cannot be stressed enough. Both provide an opportunity to gain relevant professional experience, develop professional contacts and "try on" a job and organization. While you are "trying" the job on, the host of your internship is also getting to know you, and should positions open you will already be a "known quantity." An internship or practicum is doubly critical if one doesn't have library or related experience before entering library school. Many schools will help you find an internship, but you may need to be creative to find an internship or practicum to best gain the experience you need.

Below we'll look at two librarians' internship experiences.

Bill & Melinda Gates Program

I had an internship with the Gates Foundation for a year during library school. I was paid for the time I spent working for them. They had four interns in the state of California, so there would be knowledgeable folks to

Visit Vault at **www.vault.com** for insider company profiles, expert advice, career message boards, expert resume reviews, the Vault Job Board and more.

VAULT CAREER LIBRARY

45

act as tech support and intermediaries with the Gates Foundation during the year following the installation of the granted computers.

The Gates Foundation had all of us travel to Seattle for a week of training in different aspects of the computers—from software use to networking and installation. At that time we were able to meet each other and some of the librarians from California who were also there for trainings. When we got back to California, we divided up the state between us and began to attend trainings for on-site librarians. At that time, we also helped with the trainings and the installations. My portion of the state extended from Santa Cruz to the Oregon border and a little bit inland. Some of my territory overlapped with other interns; we'd talk about who would be where and when.

Over the next year after the trainers left the state, we revisited the libraries we had helped install, and often a few more. During our visits we were able to see how the librarians were doing with their machines, and help them with problems from tech issues to use issues, since they were all public access machines. If we needed to, we'd call tech support in Seattle and get help from them.

Several things were excellent about this internship. I met librarians all over California and began networking, which has been an excellent resource for me. I learned how different library systems operate and the many different ways library systems, especially rural systems, can be run. I learned how to get around inside a computer and work with different levels of tech support. I began to learn how to help people with little computer knowledge start to use computers and help people in their libraries use the computers.

I really enjoyed the internship. Now, I work as an instructor for library skills at a junior college, but my favorite job is teaching over 50s at both the local community college community education program and through Humboldt State's Osher Lifelong Learning Institute (OLLI). A couple of jobs I've worked at over the past few years have been with systems where I helped install computers.

—*Sarah Haman*

24/7 online reference internship

My virtual library internship

This began at a conference—the Virtual Reference Desk—at which my mentor, Nancy Huling, head of reference at the University of Washington Libraries, invited me to a 24/7 users' group. While there, I heard several librarians lament about the fact that, while demand for chat reference services was spiking, HR budgets were remaining flat, and they did not know how they could staff the increased hours, especially the unattractive middle-of-the-night shifts. I was intrigued. I was already doing directed field work, and was a mercenary for any type of experience-for-credit arrangement, wanting to maximize my practical experience for my portfolio.

I approached Nancy with the idea of not only an internship but an internship program at the University of Washington, or other library schools, in which, under a librarian at a public or academic library or under a reference professor's aegis, a library student would man shifts on 24/7, have some transcript review by Susan Barb, the training director for 24/7 who does transcript review for all 24/7 librarians, and more in-depth transcript evaluation by the supervising librarian. The student would get training, experience and library school credit, and become a known quantity to the sponsoring library and to 24/7.

In many cases the supervising library, if it wasn't a library school, would have the quality control responsibility, but would gain credit for hours staffed in the 24/7 cooperative without salary expenditures. It would also get a first look at newly minted librarians. 24/7 would get additional staff for no monetary expenditure, would have the opportunity to teach the service and its merits to librarians who would graduate, and possibly have to implement virtual reference services at their new jobs, as well as get a first look at these librarians as possible employees.

Nancy was intrigued, although UW was not a co-op library at the time, and she advocated the idea to Susan McGlamery, founder of 24/7, who offered the option to a small group of iSchool students. Only I ended up doing it.

In March 2004, I started monitoring two shifts on the public queue (I was already monitoring the UW-Cornell academic queue as part of a reference directed field work). During the course of the academic quarter, I would consult Susan Barb or Nancy after the fact on transcripts I was unsure about, and as my directed field work supervisor, Nancy was to read a self-evaluation with transcript analysis on my part. I tended to overdo things and presented her with a booklet consisting of an Excel spreadsheet containing a column with every transcript in its own cell and a column next to it with my own context notes and statements on what I had done well and not so well in each chat session. I met with her for an hour and we discussed it. Then she filled out her part of the evaluation as to whether or not I had met the goals and objectives I had stated at the beginning of the quarter, and whether or not I deserved the credit hours.

Visit Vault at **www.vault.com** for insider company profiles, expert advice, career message boards, expert resume reviews, the Vault Job Board and more.

VAULT CAREER LIBRARY   **47**

I truly enjoyed my hours on the queues. I had been well prepared with beginning, advanced and digital reference courses, as well as subject reference, the Librarian's Internet Index training and the Washington State Virtual Reference course. According to Susan Barb, my patron reviews were positive. In late May 2004, I called to tell her I would be missing a shift because I had to go to my academic convocation. I apologized and said that I probably would not be eligible for my internship once I graduated, and told her I would be happy to cover my hours until she found somebody else to do so. She told me that she would like me to cover them. I was thrilled and then she said, "So I'll send you an I-9." I was stunned, and said, "you mean for money?!?!" I was hired.

—*Nicolette Warisse Sosulski, Business Librarian, Portage District Library, Portage, Mich.*

Dual Degrees

This author found herself in "library school" surrounded by history, English and education majors, and was a little embarrassed to admit what she had majored in. One day when she told a professor that she majored in business, he said, "You will be in demand because few people have the more technical degrees." Many jobs, especially in academic/university libraries may also require a second master's beyond the MLIS in a subject area. For example, an art bibliographer at a university library may also have a master's in art or art history, while a position as a Chinese language cataloger would need either an additional degree in Chinese language or fluency in Chinese. A library administrator, especially a dean of libraries, typically has a PhD in either library and information science or, more likely, higher education administration. To be a law librarian, one must not only have an MLIS but also a JD degree. Overall, the type of undergraduate or other degrees required depend on the specific position.

Other requirements

Many states require librarians to become certified after their MLIS to become a school librarian or school media specialist—certification varies from state to state. Often for school librarians or others working in the public school, a teaching certificate is also required. It is best to check with your state licensing board and the state department of education to determine what additional credentials beyond the MLIS you may need.

Exceptions to the rule

In small-town and rural public libraries, it is not unusual to find individuals without the ALA MLIS degree serving as "librarians," and in many corporate libraries it is not unusual for someone in a research department to also work in or be in charge of the corporate library or information center. In corporate libraries, you will sometimes find that the "librarian" will have a master's degree related to the business of the corporation rather than, or in addition to, an MLIS. For example, a librarian for a major oil company may have a master's degree in chemistry or petroleum engineering.

Visit Vault at **www.vault.com** for insider company profiles, expert advice, career message boards, expert resume reviews, the Vault Job Board and more.

VAULT CAREER LIBRARY   **49**

Applying for the Job

CHAPTER 5

The first thing to do before applying for positions in which you are interested is to get all of the information and materials that an application might require. Among the types of things you may be asked to include in your application, other than a cover letter and resume, are official copies of academic transcripts (for both graduate and undergraduate degrees). If you don't live in the same location where you received or are getting your degree, it's best to request official copies ahead of time.

Resumes

Most people know what a resume is. Do you need one? Definitely. Do you also need an online portfolio? Maybe. A resume, as most know, is a document which describes your experience and achievements and may be posted online and/or printed on paper. Note the use of the word "describes"—you really can't "show" your work in a resume. An online portfolio is excellent when it comes to that. Let's address the resume first.

Other than your cover letter, the resume is the most important first impression you can make. The employer or search committee is looking for a resume that stands out. Having hired or served on search committees for over 20 years, this author has seen a lot of resumes. Many are pretty generic; others are pretty horrific. It is essential that you proof read your cover letter and your resume. Typos and incorrect grammar still happen— all the time.

Required vs. preferred

Most potential employers or search committees are looking for resumes that stand out. Depending on the position, the pool you may be competing against could be quite large—but then the winnowing process begins. How do you survive that first cut? Look closely at the job announcement for the words required, preferred or desired. Let's look at the following excerpt from a job announcement:

Requirements:

• Master's degree in Library Science from a program accredited by the American Library Association required.

• Undergraduate degree in a business-related field preferred; advanced degree in a business-related field preferred.

• Two years reference experience, including experience with electronic resources, in an academic library preferred.

• Business-related experience preferred.

It begins with "requirements," but you'll note that only the first is required; the other three are preferred.

In the following example, a longer list of experience and skills are required with additional experience or knowledge preferred.

QUALIFICATIONS:

Required: Master's degree from an ALA-accredited library school or equivalent combination of education and relevant library experience. Evidence of organization and prioritization skills. Strong interpersonal and communication skills. Ability to work independently as well as in groups. Evidence of ability to set and meet production goals. Demonstrated ability to be flexible and handle detailed work.

Preferred: Library experience including use of automated library systems, preferably Voyager and OCLC. Experience with spreadsheet and database software, preferably Excel and MS Access. Supervisory experience.

The evidence they're asking for

For those required items, other than the degree, those hiring are asking for evidence and demonstrated ability. So in your resume and cover letter, make sure that you provide examples of how you meet each requirement. For example, for "strong interpersonal and communication skills," you might mention classes you have taught, public speaking experiences, committees chaired or on which you served or writing you've done, whether for publication, website content or newsletters. Address as well as possible each of the required and as many of the preferred that you can without really stretching it and coming off as vague. Since the above job announcement specifically prefers Excel and MS Access experience, if you have that experience don't bury it by saying "experience with MS Office"—spell it out. It seems so simple, but put yourself in the seat of those reviewing your application and see how fast you can find the requirements and preferred skills in your cover letter and resume. Of course, you'll be able to do it faster—you did write the resume—but make it as easy as possible for your future employer to find you.

Readability

Use a readable font and type size. Your audience, and that's what it is, may not want to spend the time wading through your resume if it's hard to read. Leave Velvenda Cooler, Minya Nouvelle and Mufferaw to your T-shirts, greeting cards, flyers and other things. It may seem stodgy but Times New Roman, Georgia, Tahoma, Century and other common fonts are easiest to read. One search committee jokingly referred to a candidate as the "goth martial arts chick" based on the font she used for her resume. They ended up interviewing her and were quite surprised that she wasn't anything like the picture they had in their heads. They also ended up hiring her, based on her interview and her qualifications, but her resume gave several pause and she might have been overlooked for that very reason. Sure, it's not exactly fair, but your cover letter and resume (and the right qualifications) get you the interview. If you're not sure how readable your resume is, have one of your professors take a look, or if possible, someone in personnel. The American Library Association's NMRT (New Members Roundtable) has a resume review service on their website at http://www.ala.org/ala/mgrps/rts/nmrt/oversightgroups/comm/resreview/re sumereview.cfm, as do many campus career centers.

In addition to using a readable font and type size, don't use various fonts in your resume. Different type sizes, yes; italics, bold and underlining, yes; but stay with the same font.

Grabbing attention

Sell yourself. A resume isn't the time to be modest (nor is it the time to be pompous). What is so special about you? Why would you be perfect for the job? This is so essential for new graduates. You don't want to appear vanilla in a group of Cherry Garcia and Chunky Monkey. The best way to immediately grab the attention of your reader is to start with a section that gives a summary, highlights or an overall picture of you. Granted, it's much easier to do this if you've got three to five years' experience, but it can be done at the entry-level.

Visit Vault at **www.vault.com** for insider company profiles, expert advice, career message boards, expert resume reviews, the Vault Job Board and more.

VAULT CAREER LIBRARY

53

If you are a recent graduate, a chronological resume is usually more practical. It's also most commonly used in public and academic library jobs. The examples that follow are chronological resumes, with one functional resume. The functional resume is more often used for corporate library jobs, especially if you are interviewing with decision-makers and other individuals who aren't librarians. In those cases, you'll want to make sure you translate your experience in layman's terms rather than just list former positions held.

Here's a "summary or overview" from an entry-level resume:

SUMMARY:

Highly proficient library specialist, with particular skills in business and government documents research using the full range of print and online reference sources. Familiarity with cataloging and collection development processes, AACR2/MARC, the LS subject headings, DDC/LCC, and various integrated library systems. Knowledge of principles of competitive intelligence and the latest Web 2.0/Library 2.0 tools, techniques and applications.

Here's an "overview" from an experienced librarian's resume:

OVERVIEW:

Over 27 years in increasingly responsible library positions with approximately 20 years in coordinator, director, or administrative positions. Have worked in or managed every function in a library. Extensive experience in choosing, procuring, licensing, implementing, and managing a variety of electronic products including databases and integrated library systems on utilizing different platforms, software, and networks. Considerable experience promoting library resources to diverse groups, managing personnel, public relations and marketing, grant writing, strategic planning, budgeting, collection development, acquisitions, public speaking, teaching and user-instruction.

Despite the similar length of these two, the first focuses partly on experience but mostly on knowledge and familiarity, while the second focuses only on experience.

What's your objective?

If you look at a dozen resume books, you will probably find recommendations that you start the resume with an objective. It's good for you to know what your objective is, but it's really not necessary to put it on your resume. The beginning of your resume is prime real estate and should be more wisely used with a summary that tells the reader why you are so special and perfectly qualified for the job. But if you do have an objective on your resume that is specific, such as "To become a science subject specialist in an academic library," you must change it if you apply for a position in a public or corporate library. Whether or not a science specialist is your dream job, nothing will stop a potential employer more quickly (other than misspellings and bad grammar) than reading an objective that doesn't match the job she is looking to fill. Since we aren't in the day of typewriters and print shops, there's really no reason why you can't customize a resume for each job.

Visit Vault at **www.vault.com** for insider company profiles, expert advice, career message boards, expert resume reviews, the Vault Job Board and more.

VAULT CAREER LIBRARY   55

Sample Entry-Level Resume (Chronological)

Eliza Marie Sommer

329 Matila Avenue

Tampa, FL

emsommer@lis.iu.edu

404–543–0000

OVERVIEW

Experience providing reference service to students and faculty in two different types of academic libraries including virtual reference using OCLC Questionpoint, teaching information literacy classes, searching and teaching scholarly databases, with collection development and web development. Team player with strong service orientation.

EDUCATION

Indiana University SLIS, MLS   Spring 2009 (anticipated)

Murray State University, BA   2003

EXPERIENCE

TAMPA COMMUNITY COLLEGE   2008–present

Intern

- Assist students, faculty and community members in identifying and locating sources of information and to use library technology effectively.
- Teach information literacy instruction sessions.
- Create online subject guides in LibGuides.
- Perform statewide collection development.
- Evaluate print collection and run statistical reports on library databases.
- Perform other duties as requested.

UNIVERSITY OF SOUTH FLORIDA   2008–present

Reference Assistant

- Answer reference and directional questions via e-mail, telephone and online chat.
- Create and edit pathfinders for Walden University student use.
- Apply familiarity with scholarly databases, online resources, QuestionPoint and Lotus Notes.

IU BLOOMINGTON   2007–2008

Graduate Assistant

- Run literature searches and create course web pages.
- Collect online data for research both manually and by writing appropriate computer scripts.
- Perform other duties as requested.

UNIVERSITY OF NORTH CAROLINA, STATE DATA CENTER   2006–2007

Researcher

- Work independently to code computer program for locating CpG islands in silico.
- Present my own work and others' research articles.
- Edit research articles for mentor before publication, checking for spelling, grammar and clarity.

BARNES AND NOBLE   2003–2006

Bookseller

- Assist customers with locating merchandise, place special orders, carry out retail transactions.
- Recommend books to readers of all ages.
- Work individually with struggling young readers.

SKILLS

- Teaching Experience
- Excellent Communication and Customer Service Skills
- Web development and design skills
- Familiar with C++, Java, SQL, Perl, XHTML, CSS, basic Unix
- Basic proficiency with Adobe Flash
- Comfortable in Microsoft Office Suite on Macs and PCs
- Reading and writing simple French

INVOLVEMENT

- Web Master, Indiana University Student Chapter, 2008-present
- Member, School of Library and Information Science Curriculum Steering Committee, 2007–2008

REFERENCES

DR. LOUIS FRANKE

Indiana University SLIS

505–374–2989

frankl@slis.iu.edud

MARY MILLER

Head of Reference

University of South Florida

404–878–0394

mmiller@usf.edu

DEB STEWART

Head of Public Services

Tampa Community College

404–999–3432

dastewart@tcc.lib.fl.us

Sample Experienced Resume (Chronological)

DEBORAH A. SOMMER

317 Metropolis Street

Metropolis, IL 62960

618–524–0000

dsommer@shawls.lib.il.us

OVERVIEW

Over 27 years in increasingly responsible library positions with approximately 20 years in coordinator, director, or administrative positions. Have worked in or managed every function in a library. Extensive experience in choosing, procuring, licensing, implementing, and managing a variety of electronic products including databases and integrated library systems utilizing different platforms, software, and networks. Considerable experience promoting library resources to diverse groups, managing personnel, public relations and marketing, grant writing, strategic planning, budgeting, collection development and acquisitions, public speaking, teaching and user-instruction.

EXPERIENCE

METROPOLIS PUBLIC LIBRARY   2008–present

Director

- Serve as the Chief Executive officer of the Library, under the direction of the Board of Trustees
- Responsible for the functioning of the library as a whole including personnel management, evaluation and scheduling, budget control, programming, publicity, grant writing and development of new electronic resources

METROPOLIS PUBLIC LIBRARY   February 2008–July 2008

Part-time Librarian

- Worked the Circulation Desk
- Assisted patrons in finding materials
- Planned and conducted story hours
- Developed programs for students
- Taught beginning computer classes to senior citizens
- Developed a new website
- Held gaming nights

OCLC QUESTIONPOINT. VIRTUAL ONLINE REFERENCE CHAT SERVICE   2006–

Independent Contractor

- Work 15–25 hours a week providing online reference service to answer queries posed by patrons from public and academic libraries as part of a nationwide library consortium in chat format using 24/7 reference system

WALKER MANAGEMENT LIBRARY

Owen Graduate School of Management, Vanderbilt University, Nashville, Tenn.   2000–2007

Instruction and Collection Librarian
- Worked closely with the faculty and students of the Owen Graduate School of Management and others in the University community to promote and provide library services including in-person and online consultation and reference services
- Administered the Library's instruction program
- Evaluated the collection and selected materials for purchase
- Wrote and developed instructional and promotional materials as well as web content
- Implemented and managed the faculty research database and faculty research services

WALKER MANAGEMENT LIBRARY

Owen Graduate School of Management, Vanderbilt University, Nashville, Tenn.   2003–2005

Director
- Managed the budget and collections of the library to provide services to the students and faculty of the MBA, MS Finance and PhD in Business programs
- Oversaw the Access Services, Information Services and BIS (service for corporate clients). Hired, supervised and evaluated 5 librarians and 5 support staff.
- Selected books, journals and electronic resources to support the research and curriculum of the School
- Marketed the library to students and faculty; taught workshops and spoke to classes; served on the Dean's Scholarship Committee and numerous inter-library committees

NATIONAL NETWORK OF LIBRARIES OF MEDICINE

(contract position funded by the National Library of Medicine)

Lottes Health Sciences Library, University of Missouri–Columbia   2001–2003

Regional Library Improvement Coordinator and Missouri Outreach Librarian
- Served as the membership coordinator of over 350 medical libraries in 6 states
- Taught Medline and DOCLINE classes to librarians
- Held workshops for physicians and medical students
- Taught consumer health workshops in public libraries
- Wrote grants
- Served as technical advisor
- Development strategic plans
- Member of the team that initiated the Missouri Medline "Go Local" database
- Developed web content and provided information to public and rural health agencies

(GS–13) USDA FOREST SERVICE

Southern Region. Adjunct Librarian III, University of Georgia Libraries   1992–2000

Administrative Librarian

- Oversaw the information center that served the practitioners and researchers in 13 southern states
- Managed budget, developed strategic plans, supervised two offices–the INFOSouth information service in Athens, GA and the cataloging and database unit in the Atlanta Regional office
- Collaborated with the national network of Forest Service libraries to implement a new integrated library system (SIRSI)
- Developed website and online reference services

SBDC CONNECTION

(a nationwide library serving all Small Business Development Centers nationwide)

University of Georgia, Small Business Development Center, Athens, GA   1988–1992

Director

- Started the first nationwide information service to serve the Small Business Development Centers nationwide
- Managed a budget of over $400,000 supervised two librarians, two support staff and 5 student workers
- Promoted services to users, taught workshops and made presentations at the annual national meeting
- Developed a database of small business information publications searchable via the internet (pre-Web)
- Worked with the Technology Transfer and Small Business Incubation programs

UNIVERSITY OF GEORGIA LIBRARIES

Main Library Reference Department

User Education Coordinator   1985–1988

Business and general Reference Librarian, Librarian II   1983–1987

- Provided general and business reference service and online searches
- Coordinated the instruction program, taught classes and workshops, development library guides and instructional handouts, selected business sources for the reference collection and taught the University 101 freshman course

UNIVERSITY OF NORTH CAROLINA AT WILMINGTON

Randall Library   1981–1983

Online Service Coordinator/Assistant Reference Librarian. Assistant Professor

- Provided reference service to students and faculty
- Served as the liaison with the School of Business
- Implemented an online search service and taught instruction classes

EDUCATION

Owen Executive Leadership Certificate   2007
24 hours coursework

Coursework, PhD program, University of Missouri   2000–2003

Master of Science in Library Science. University of Tennessee, Knoxville, Tenn   1980

Bachelor of Science in Business. Murray State University, Murray, Kentucky   1977

AWARDS

Herbert Schooling Graduate Student Award, College of Education   2001–2002

Graduate Assistantship, Educational Leadership and Policy Analysis Department,
School of Education, University of Missouri–Columbia   2001

Certificate of Merit, USDA Forest Service, "For Sustained Superior Performance"   1999
(Cash award $2000)

Certificate of Merit, USDA Forest Service, "For Sustained Superior Performance" 1998
(Cash award $2000)

Certificate of Merit, USDA Forest Service, "For Superior Performance Managing
INFOSouth and FS INFO Library Services"   1996
(Cash award of $1500)

Certificate of Merit, USDA Forest Service, "For Excellence in Providing Library
and Information Services to Region 8 and the Southern Research Station and taking
a leadership role in the FS INFO Network"   1995
(Cash award of $2800)

GRANTS (SELECTED)

Consultant, "Excellence in Public Health and School Health Nursing: Utilizing Information to
Improve Practice." Internet Access to Digital Libraries proposal to the National Library of
Medicine. February 1, 2003. Awarded $25,000 by the National Library of Medicine.

Co-Author, "Developing a Regional Cooperative Database to "GO LOCAL." Connecting
Local Consumer Health Resources to the National Medline plus Database." January 31, 2003.
Awarded $50,000 by the National Library of Medicine.

Consultant, "Health Resources for Area Health Education Center (AHEC) Community
Preceptors." Mid-Missouri AHEC. Awarded $133,000 for Phase I by the National Library of
Medicine. October 1, 2002.

Technical Advisor, "Enhancing Assess to Biomedical Information via Ariel." Kansas State University, Veterinary Medical Library. Awarded $10,000 by the National Library of Medicine. May 1, 2002

Author and Project Director, "Small Business Information Clearinghouse." December 1, 1988. Awarded $250,000 by the U.S. Small Business Administration.

PRESENTATIONS AND PUBLICATIONS (SELECTED)

Instructor, Beginning Computer Classes –Metropolis Public Library

Co-author, "The Embedded Librarian: Librarian in the Classroom" paper presented at the Annual LOEX (Library Instruction) conference, San Diego, CA 2007. Accepted for publication, forthcoming in The Teaching Librarian.

Moderator, The Peabody Library Leadership Institute. Vanderbilt University. 2006 and 2007.

Instructor, "Financial and Investment Resources on the Web." Summer Retirement & Elder-hostel seminar, Vanderbilt University, 2003–2006.

Instructor and Planner of numerous business information related workshops to MBA students, faculty and alumni. 2003–2007.

Invited Presenter, "Teaching Adult Learners." Joint meeting of the South Dakota Library Association and the Mid-Continent Medical Libraries Association, Annual Conference, Sioux Falls, SD 2003

Instructor, "Consumer Health Resources." A public workshop for seniors. Taught this workshop 20 times in various locations in Missouri, Nebraska, Kansas and Colorado. 2002–2003.

Presenter, "A Strategy for Regional Licensing of Electronic Resources." Joint meeting of the Regional Advisory Committee of the National Network of Libraries of Medicine, and the Directors of Health Sciences Resource Libraries in the Mid-continent Region. Salt Lake City, UT 2003.

Instructor, "Finding and Evaluating Quality Consumer Health Information on the Web." Presented 2002 and 2003 as in-service training for public librarians (Kansas City and St. Louis).

Presenter, "Collaborative Borrowing Agreements among International Forestry Collection Libraries." Meeting of the Pacific Northwest Group of Canadian Forestry Librarians, Victoria, British Columbia, Canada, 1999.

"The World Wide Web: Forestry Applications." Southern Forest Health Conference, Clemson, SC, January 1996.

"The World Wide Web: What's in it for Foresters?" IN: Journal of Forestry. With Carol C. Green. December 1995.

Instructor, "Resources for Recreation." Recreation Short Course, Clemson University, Clemson, SC, September 1992, 1993, 1994.

Presenter, "Non-Library Small Business Resources." BRASS (Business Reference Sources and Services Division) Program. American Library Association, Annual Conference, Atlanta, GA June 1991.

"Proposed Methodology of Performance Appraisal of Bibliographic Instruction Librarians." In: Performance Appraisal in Reference Services in ARL Libraries. Washington, DC: Office of Management Studies, Association of Research Libraries, Systems and Procedures Exchange Center. Kit 139, November-December 1987. pp. 49–60.

Instructor, Business Reference Workshops (four sessions), UGA Libraries, August– September 1985. Repeated September 1986.

Co-presenter, "Teaching the Research Paper: The Library Component". Conference on College Composition and Communication, Detroit, Michigan, 1983. With Sylvia Welborn.

CONTINUING EDUCATION (SELECTED)

Social Networking Tools for Public Libraries, Shawnee Library Association	2008
Gaming in Libraries Workshop, Lewis & Clark Library Association	2008
E-Rate Workshop, Shawnee Library Association	2008
Leadership Institute for Academic Librarians, Harvard University	2004
Numerous training sessions for different online full text magazine, newspaper and journal databases.	
"Focus Group Interviewing: A Qualitative Research Method for the Library." 8 hour Credit Course, Medical Library Association, Salt Lake City	2002
MU Health Sciences Library Workshop. "Power point Update."	2002
"Introduction to Web-enhanced Instruction." The Center for Scholarship in Teaching and Learning, Southeast Missouri State University	2001
"Teaching Enhancement Workshop." The Center for Scholarship in Teaching and Learning, Southeast Missouri State University	2000
"Instructional Design I." The Center for Scholarship in Teaching and Learning, Southeast Missouri State University	2000
"Financial Management for Natural Resource Managers." Regional Training Institute, (one week course), St. Louis, MO	1998

Visit Vault at **www.vault.com** for insider company profiles, expert advice, career message boards, expert resume reviews, the Vault Job Board and more.

VAULT CAREER LIBRARY

63

"Supervisory Management in the Federal Workplace." (two week course),
USDA Government University, Lancaster, PA   1997

"Federal Webmasters Conference," Bethesda, MD   1995

"Oracle programming course" (2 weeks) Denver, Colorado   1994

Association of Research Libraries, Office of Management Studies,
"Analytical Skills Workshop." Athens, Georgia   1988

North Carolina Special Libraries Association Conference, (CEU)
"Information for Economic Progress," Greensboro, North Carolina   1987

"Management in State and Local Government." Levels I, II, and III,
Athens, Georgia   1983 and 1984

PROFESSIONAL MEMBERSHIPS

American Library Association   1980–present

Medical Library Association   2001–2004

Mid-continent Medical Library Association   2001–2004

Special Libraries Association   1989–2006

Sample Functional Resume

DEBORAH A. SOMMER

317 Metropolis Street
Metropolis, IL 62960
618–524–0000
dsommer@shawls.lib.il.us

OVERVIEW

- Over 28 years professional library experience
- Extensive experience with personnel management, budgeting and grant writing
- Proficient with online library systems, databases and computers
- Extensive public relations and marketing experience
- Experience teaching library literacy and information workshops
- Excellent customer service and communication skills

RELEVANT EXPERIENCE

LIBRARY MANAGEMENT

- Developed and administered budgets in excess of $1 million
- Managed facilities
- Developed long-term strategic plans
- Developed and implemented technology plans

PERSONNEL MANAGEMENT

- Supervised and evaluated professionals and support staff in academic and special libraries
- Hired and trained librarians, support staff and student workers
- Recruited top candidates for positions

REFERENCE AND INFORMATION SERVICE

- Served as business, natural resources and health sciences subject specialist in academic and special libraries
- Assisted library users in searching databases
- Met with students or faculty in research consulations
- Provided in-person, phone, email and virtual reference to student, faculty and researchers

TEACHING AND TRAINING

- Taught computer classes, subject-specific internet classes, information literacy, library use and computer use to students and users of all ages
- Trained library staff in computer use, databases and other computerized information resources
- Taught workshops on how to efficiently search the internet
- Developed and taught workshops on finding consumer health information; online investment resources; small business information and other topics

OTHER

- Designed and managed website for libraries
- Selected materials for academic and public library collections
- Procured and negotiated licenses for electronic resources

Visit Vault at **www.vault.com** for insider company profiles, expert advice,
career message boards, expert resume reviews, the Vault Job Board and more.

V∧ULT CAREER LIBRARY

65

- Wrote grants, secured funding from library agencies and the federal government to support library programs
- Developed Gaming programs in public libraries
- Managed library contract catalogers performing retrospective conversion
- Chose and implemented integrated library systems

JOB HISTORY

- **Library Director**, Metropolis Public Library. 2008–

- **Part-time Librarian**, Metropolis Public Library. 2008

- **Virtual Reference Librarian**, OCLC Questionpoint. 2006–

- **Library Director (2003-2005), Collection Librarian and Instruction Coordinator**, Walker Management Library, Vanderbilt University. 2003–2007

- **Outreach Services Librarian**, National Network of Libraries of Medicine, Health Sciences Library, University of Missouri-Columbia. 2000–2003

- **Administrative Librarian**, U.S. Forest Service, Region 8, Atlanta, GA. 1992–2000

- **Library Director**, Small Business Development Center, University of Georgia. Athens Georgia. 1988–1992

- **Reference Librarian and User Education Coordinator**, Main Reference Department, University of Georgia Libraries. 1983–1988

- **Reference Librarian**, University of North Carolina-Wilmington. 1981–1983

EDUCATION

- M.L.I.S., Library and Information Science, University of Tennessee. 1980

- B.S., Business Administration, Murray State University. 1977

There are hundreds of resume guides both in print and online. The sample resumes shown here are examples only. There isn't just one way to do a resume. The key is to have one that shows your experience as it relates to the positions for which you are applying, one that is easy to read and that gives you a showcase for your knowledge, skills and abilities.

Public Library: Sample Job Listing

Job announcement: Librarian, business services

Job Details: The Business Librarian provides vision and strategic leadership for business reference and services at the City District Library through the planning and implementation of business-related programming in library and outreach settings.

This position will work to create a welcoming, positive, and dynamic experience for business researchers, small business owners and students in the library setting. Candidates must be customer-service-oriented, flexible, community-minded and relate well to both students and business persons. This position involves a flexible schedule, to include evenings and weekends. Travel will be required to and from library and outreach locations.

Qualified candidates must possess:

• MLS from an ALA approved institution

• One or more years of experience in providing high-quality service to the public

• Working knowledge of Microsoft Windows and Office software

Additional desired skills

• Business programming experience

• Knowledge of business information sources

• Staff training experience

Successful candidates should demonstrate:

• Excellent organizational ability and customer service skills

• Flexibility, detail focus, and ability to prioritize and deal with ambiguity

• Excellent oral, communication and interpersonal skills

Visit Vault at **www.vault.com** for insider company profiles, expert advice, career message boards, expert resume reviews, the Vault Job Board and more.

V\ULT CAREER LIBRARY

67

- Ability to work collaboratively in a team environment

- Ability to solve problems creatively

- Ability to effectively build partnerships and promote the benefits of change in a culture that values diversity of opinion and historic precedent

Resumes (including three references and salary expectations) may be submitted via mail or e-mail by August 18, 2009 to:

John Johns
Business Manager
City District Library
300 Library Lane
Big City, OH 00342

This description is not all-inclusive. If you meet the minimum qualifications and would like to learn more, please contact Human Resources.

Public Library: Sample Resume

This resume is a good fit for the entry-level public library position described above.

Nicolette Warisse Sosulski

123 Main Street, Apt. B.
Portage, MI 49027
Phone: 572–820–0000
nwsosulski@uwsil.edu

SUMMARY OF QUALIFICATIONS

Experience as a reference librarian in personal and digital environments. Experience serving academic and public library patrons in desk, chat, e-mail and phone platforms. Level II Librarian's Professional Certificate, Library of Michigan.

LIBRARY PROFESSIONAL EXPERIENCE

- **24/7 Reference, www.247ref.org**

  3/04–present. Digital Reference Librarian. Answer queries posed by patrons from public and academic libraries as part of a nationwide library consortium in chat format using 24/7 reference system.

  From 3/04–6/04 served as a reference intern.
  Currently employed as staff reference librarian.

- **Small District Library, Town, OH**

  7/05–present. Substitute Librarian. Provide support to adult and children's reference desks and AnswerLine services.

- **Reference and Research Services Division, Suzzallo Library, University of Washington Libraries**

  10/03–08/04. Directed Field Work, Reference Librarian. Assisted University of Washington patrons in desk, chat (also including Cornell University patron assistance), and e-mail environments using 24/7 and QuestionPoint reference systems. Performed retrospective collection development evaluation of the reference collection in library and information science. Taught resources/research strategies workshop for course on the geography of world hunger.

- **The Internet Public Library, www.ipl.org**

  04/03–present. Digital Reference Librarian. Answer patron inquiries on wide variety of subjects in e-mail format using QRC reference system.

- **The Information School, University of Washington**

  9/02–6/04. Graduate Assistant. As part of merit-based award position, supported three to six faculty members concurrently, coordinating a variety of simultaneous projects.

Visit Vault at **www.vault.com** for insider company profiles, expert advice, career message boards, expert resume reviews, the Vault Job Board and more.

VAULT CAREER LIBRARY

69

Conducted literature reviews and supplied other research support for projects, including an investigation into reference curricula across North America and a large survey of community information behavior (IMLS grant)

OTHER LIBRARY ACTIVITIES

Conference Presentation. Virtual Reference Desk Conference, San Francisco, CA, November 2005. Presentation Title: Polysynchronous Patrons—A look at reference strategies for serving multiple virtual patrons simultaneously.

Conference Session Coordinator. Washington Library Association/Pacific Northwest Library Association Joint Conference, Wenatchee, WA, August 2004. Coordinated session on consumer health reference for the National Libraries of Medicine.

Student to Staff Representative Scholarship. American Library Association National Conference, Orlando, FL, June 2004. Supported the Campaign for America's Libraries.

Conference Assistant
- Virtual Reference Desk Conference, Cincinnati, OH, November 2004
- Public Library Association Biannual Conference, Seattle, WA, February 2004
- Virtual Reference Desk Conference, San Antonio, TX, November 2003
- NSF Information and Data Management (IDM) Workshop "Information Retrieval and Databases: Synergies and Syntheses," Seattle, WA, September 2003

Volunteer. Winchell Elementary School Library, Kalamazoo, MI; Friends of Portage District Library, Portage, MI, March 2004-present

EDUCATION

Master of Library and Information Science
University of Washington, Seattle, WA, 2004
Study included courses in Reference, Information Behavior, Classification and Cataloging, Information Systems, Library Management, Community Analysis and Preservation.

Bachelor of Arts, English Literature and Government
Georgetown University, Washington, DC, 1985.
Additional concentration in French and Spanish. Graduate courses in English Literature.

Academic Library: Sample Job Listing

Job announcement for academic library position

Digital Services Librarian, University of Smith, Smithfield, MA

POSITION TITLE: Digital Services Librarian

CATEGORY: Librarian Faculty I, Full-time

RESPONSIBILITIES: The Digital Services Librarian maintains SFX and ResearchPort, including knowledgebase maintenance, upgrade testing, and troubleshooting through individual work and coordination with the University of Smith's Information Technology Division. Specific responsibilities include:

- Providing technical assistance to library patrons via telephone and email, and writing user documentation

- Performing library Website, database gateway, authentication system, and database access maintenance and development in cooperation with the Systems Librarian and Library Web Specialist

- Participating on project teams and working on projects related to improving the library's online services, as well as participating on library teams as required to improving, evaluating, and promoting overall library services and initiatives

- Performing other job-related duties as assigned

QUALIFICATIONS: Requires a MLS from an ALA accredited university; and internship or one year position experience working with Web development and/or library systems; proficiency with HTML and HTML editors (DreamWeaver preferred); ability to quickly and effectively proof and troubleshoot Web content; proficiency with Windows and Windows-based applications; familiarity with basic UNIX commands, FTP, and an understanding of database design and use; Candidates with working knowledge of the Ex Libris integrated library systems and associated technologies such as SFX, ResearchPort, and Verde; experience working in an academic library; hands-on knowledge of the development and maintenance of database-driven Websites; familiarity with bibliographic databases and academic library database vendors; working knowledge of learning management systems such as Blackboard or WebCT; experience with Web programming languages/platforms (for example, PHP, Perl, Cold

Visit Vault at **www.vault.com** for insider company profiles, expert advice, career message boards, expert resume reviews, the Vault Job Board and more.

V∧ULT CAREER LIBRARY   **71**

Fusion, JavaScript, XML) for design of dynamic Web pages; project management experience and/or experience planning and implementing library systems are preferred.

Academic Library: Sample Resume

Jane Smith

100 Wisconsin Street NW

Washington, D.C. 20008

815.793.0000

jsmith231@yahoo.com

PROFESSIONAL EXPERIENCE AND RELATED ACTIVITIES

Digital Reference Team Intern

Library of Congress January–June 2008

- Answer general reference questions as assigned through the OCLC QuestionPoint system
- Review, fact check, and perform research for the Today in History feature of the website to maintain integrity of content
- Research and compile Web Bibliographic Guides for the states in order to facilitate access to the Library's collections

Webmaster

UK School of Library and Information Science March 2008–present

- Work closely with the Dean to regularly update, create, and maintain web content through content management system
- Spearheaded a major redesign of the School website
- Developed and executed a usability testing plan

PROFICIENCIES

- Reference experience with emphasis on: electronic resources, special collections, history and social science
- Computer help desk experience
- Formal instruction in information literacy theories and practice and experience in instructional plan design and execution
- Proficient searcher of electronic databases
- Adept at web design, usability testing and social computing (podcasting, blogging, wiki creation)
- Website development and maintenance
- Worked with database gateways, authentication systems and access maintenance

ADDITIONAL EXPERIENCE

Researcher, American Enterprise Institute, August 2000-August 2007, Washington, D.C.,
Researched and drafted position papers; conducted surveys; performed statistical analyses

EDUCATION

Masters in Library and Information Science
Catholic University of America, Washington D.C., Expected Dec. 2008

Bachelors of Arts in Government and International Studies
Oberlin College, Oberlin, OH, 2001

AFFILIATIONS

American Library Association, ASIS&T, Special Libraries Association

SKILLS

- UNIX
- Dreamweaver
- Macromedia Flash
- XHTML
- CSS
- OCLC QuestionPoint
- Windows XP/2000
- Mac OSX
- Audacity
- Adobe Photoshop
- Podcasting
- Social Networking Applications
- Microsoft Office Suite
- OpenOffice

Visit Vault at **www.vault.com** for insider company profiles, expert advice,
career message boards, expert resume reviews, the Vault Job Board and more.

VAULT CAREER LIBRARY

73

Corporate Library: Sample Job Listing

Corporate library job announcement

Knowledge manager

- Develop and implement a plan to capture, organize, archive, index, and make accessible the knowledge resources of the firm including internal work products (client files, resource materials, proposals, reports, correspondence, etc.), industry materials, competitive intelligence information, files on philanthropy and related documentation.

- Act as administrator of the firm's electronic document management database (iManage) and develop a structure for database accessibility by the firm's senior staff.

- Oversee a strategy for scanning documents for both archival files and current accessibility as resource materials for the firm's staff. • Organize data from client audits in accessible, easily retrievable resource files.

- Maintain current industry awareness by reviewing media sources for articles related to nonprofit development and philanthropy.

- Oversee weekly news clipping resource for distribution to all staff.

- Respond to reference and in-depth research requests from consultants and other staff using electronic and print resources.

- Oversee management of library and subscriptions—books, magazines, newsletters and periodicals. Develop best practice research processes and templates.

NOTES: Local residents preferred (no relocation). Salary is commensurate with background and experience. Cover letter required. The company is a full-service philanthropic management consulting firm with more than 45 years of experience and an international clientele. Letters of interest with resume should be sent to Jane Doe, Senior Vice President, Consulting Services; Big City, 1000 Main Street.

Corporate Library: Sample Resume

JOHN SMITH

82nd and 4th Avenue
Apt. 598
Chicago, IL 60631
773.483.0000
johnsmith@southeastr.com

OBJECTIVE

A team-oriented position where I can contribute my skills at research, data organization, and management to information projects, such as knowledge management and/or a corporate library.

OVERVIEW

Have managed data and content management projects organizing, developing access and retrieval of company documents; administered company's electronic document database; managed electronic document archival program; provided industry information research to clients; and responded to research requests from clients.

JOB EXPERIENCE

2006	**Assistant Library Director**, Knowledge Management, Inc., Chicago, IL
2001–2006	**Head Librarian**, Southeast Research, Atlanta, GA
2000–2001	**Content Producer/Information Scientist**, Company Name., Boston, MA
1995–1998	**Librarian**, Simmons Healthcare Corporation, Chicago, IL

EDUCATION

1995	**Simmons College**, M.L.S. *Boston, MA*
	Graduate School of Library and Information Science
1984	**Oberlin College**, B.A. *Oberlin, OH*

SOFTWARE EXPERIENCE

Proficient in:
Dialog (Classic and Web), Microsoft Office suite (Word, Access, Excel), Netscape Communicator suite (Navigator, Composer), Internet search tools and browsers, Emacs, HTML

Additional experience:
XML, Lotus Notes, OCLC system, RapidSQL, Embarcadero ER Studio, Visio, HTML Pro, Front Page, dBase III and IV

PROFESSIONAL MEMBERSHIPS

Special Libraries Association
Illinois Library Association
American Libraries Association.

References: *Furnished Upon Request*

Visit Vault at **www.vault.com** for insider company profiles, expert advice,
career message boards, expert resume reviews, the Vault Job Board and more.

V/\ULT CAREER LIBRARY

75

Advice on Cover Letters

Length

There are differing opinions about the length of cover letters and resumes. The general consensus is to keep them each to one page. However, if there is substantive information relevant to the position you are applying for, the cover letter and the resume should reflect that, even if it exceeds one page. Someone with years of relevant experience or one who's been in the field for a number of years will definitely have a multipage resume. Be sure, though, to keep the cover letter and resume as concise as possible and avoid being redundant, spinning the same information in different ways. Avoid using hard to read fonts or unusual ones, and set the type size for 12.

Introduction

You should address your letter to the person named in the job advertisement or announcement, or if no person is named it is safe to address it to the search committee or library director (his name can easily be found by checking the website). The first paragraph should be an introduction, where you state that you are writing to express your interest in the position. Be very careful to list the correct title of the position as listed in the job announcement.

Customizing your approach

If you are applying for a lot of jobs, don't send a generic letter. Customize your letter for each position. Some will advise to state where you saw the position advertised, but that's only a suggestion. You should offer a brief introduction of why you think you would make an excellent candidate for the position. Focus on professional assets only. Do not say that you wish to "relocate" to the area to be closer to family or your fiancée, or that you read a book about Montana and always wanted to live there. Those may be some of your legitimate reasons but they aren't of interest to the employer or search committee. Things of that nature may come out in the interview in less formal settings.

Emphasize your skills

The next paragraphs need to address each element of the job description. You should expand upon your introduction, and focus on the minimum and preferred requirements of the position. Don't make a search committee or prospective employer hunt to find that you meet the minimum requirements, or meet the preferred or desired requirements. As briefly as possible, give a couple of examples that illustrate your experience and refer to items on your resume for further information. If the position requires web skills or experience developing promotional materials, if you have examples of website development refer to the website address and list it on your resume.

Closing

The last paragraph should state how you look forward to an opportunity to meet with the contact person to discuss your experiences and qualifications. Reiterate the phone number(s) where you can be reached, and state that you have attached your resume to the letter. That statement may seem obvious but letters and resumes occasionally become separated. Close with: "Thank you for your consideration and I look forward to discussing this position with you further."

Sample Cover Letter

The following cover letter is for an entry-level, public library position.

John Johns
Business Manager
City District Library
300 Library Lane
Big City, OH 00342

Dear Mr. Jones:

I am writing in reference to your opening for the business librarian position at the City District Library. I received my master's degree in library and information science at the Information School of the University of Washington in June 2004, concentrating my course work and extracurricular experiences in reference and research services.

My practical knowledge and experience in reference started with work on the Internet Public Library in my class with John Smith, continued with a course in digital reference, and grew through directed field work and on-the-job experience. Since March 2004, I have worked as a digital reference librarian covering queues for national public library and academic library consortia for the 24/7 Reference Project, now affiliated with OCLC. Member libraries include the Boston (Mass.), Baltimore County, (Md.), Rochester (N.H.), Boise (Idaho), Johnson County (Kan.), Los Angeles and San Francisco (Calif.) public libraries.

Although my work history does include a large amount of digital experience, I love the more traditional mode of reference service, and served faculty, students and the general public working on the reference desk of the Suzzallo Library at the University of Washington. As a substitute librarian at the Main Street Public Library, I have enjoyed serving patrons at the different service desks here.

My library and information science education was financed by a competitive award to work as a graduate assistant at the University of Washington. Through this experience as a member of Professor Jane Smith's research team, I became inspired by the role that the public library has the potential to play in the larger community. In order to grow in librarianship outside my reference activities with patrons, I pursued course work in community analysis and collection development to increase my success in that arena. I was fortunate enough to have opportunities to use these courses immediately. I was part of a team that developed a community information web page for new mothers of Small County, Washington. I also gained practical experience in collection development when I evaluated the science reference collection at Jones Library.

I enjoy teaching. During my time as a graduate assistant, on my own initiative, I developed a training program for graduate assistants that made its debut in fall 2003, and has been continued at the Information School. It included a five-hour class I designed and taught, and gave me experience in classroom teaching and curricular design in addition to the one-on-one information literacy and bibliographic instruction elements.

Though your position advertised is that of a business librarian associate, circumstances while I was at the Information School precluded my enrolling in courses in business reference or competitive intelligence there. I did take legal research and government documents courses, which are extremely helpful in addressing some business inquiries. I have tried to make a point of increasing my business reference subject knowledge by joining ALA's BRASS (Business Reference Sources and Services), and attending their programs and using their resources. I have found business areas of knowledge very interesting since my days as an academic administrator at the University of Chicago, where I had regular interactions with the MBA program, and worked in the office of financial planning and budget. As a librarian working for the 24/7 reference service, I frequently receive questions on business topics. Some of the consortia served are the Delaware state and public libraries, and because of this we get a large number of questions on business registration procedures from all over the country, since basing a business in Delaware has substantial advantages in some areas. Further, since our patron base includes students studying for undergraduate and graduate degrees in business administration, I do have familiarity with many business databases and resources. If I am fortunate to be placed in this position, I will, of course, use all means possible to extend my knowledge in this area.

The City District Library's array of programs and services is impressive, reflecting an institution committed to reaching out to all facets of its patron community. Since moving here and using your library, I have observed the friendly and supportive work environment that exists there. I would consider it a privilege to work at your library, and hope for the chance to discuss this opportunity with you further. I can be reached at (572) 820-0000. Thank you in advance for your consideration.

Sincerely,

Jane Doe

Visit Vault at **www.vault.com** for insider company profiles, expert advice, career message boards, expert resume reviews, the Vault Job Board and more.

VAULT CAREER LIBRARY

79

References

One of the most critical things you need to have, other than your resume, is a list of individuals who will serve as your references. Choose your references wisely. These people need to be familiar with your academic performance as well as your job performance. Typically, applications require a minimum of three references. Of the three, if at all possible, it's a good idea to have two who can address (favorably) your library-related work and one who can address your academic performance.

After making a list of potential references, contact them. Never, ever list someone as a reference unless you have spoken to him or her first. Recognize that it can take considerable time for your references to write the letters, so plan for that. Some job announcements ask for the names and contact information for your references, while some ask you to send the letters with your application. Reference letters that address your qualifications for a specific position are ideal. (Show your gratitude to the individuals who are writing these letters. A thank-you note is appropriate for the first letter. However, if someone has written a number of different letters of recommendation for you, you may want to consider a tasteful, not necessarily expensive, gift.) Don't forget to include your references' phone numbers and e-mails, because today many employers prefer to request letters this way.

As for the phone number, many libraries are calling your references with a specific list of questions. Will a potential employer call individuals not on your reference list? She certainly will. If it is obvious that you have excluded your current immediate supervisor from your reference list, he may receive a call asking about your work. What do you do about your employer finding out that you are job hunting? Of course, the best practice would be to let him know. If you are a new or soon-to-be new graduate, your employer should expect that you are job hunting. However, if you are already in your second professional library position, it can be dicey if your relationship isn't good with your immediate supervisor. You don't want to be treated differently because "you already have one foot out the door"— because you may end up staying. If you don't include your immediate supervisor as a reference, include something on your resume or cover letter that states that you'd prefer your supervisor not be contacted unless you are being considered as a serious candidate for the position.

Online Portfolios

Now that you've nailed your resume and understand how to customize it and your cover letter for each position, it's time to polish your online portfolio. What is an online portfolio? One thing an online portfolio isn't is just a resume posted online. An online portfolio is closer to a personal, but professional, website. It's becoming more common among recent graduates, and not necessarily just among those aiming toward a technical position. Yes, it is a place to demonstrate your design skills and html coding, but it's much more.

Consider this—you are a product. Your online portfolio is a way to sell yourself to potential buyers (employers). When buying a new coffee maker some people will just go to the store and buy one. Others may ask people about their experience with X coffee maker, read reviews and comparisons online and then look for the best price. Your online portfolio backs up your cover letter and resume for those employers who want as much information about you as possible before they buy (or invite you for an interview). It provides a place where one can share more details about work experience than is practical on a resume; it's a place where you can elaborate on, describe or show the results of projects worked on; a place to make your presentations and papers accessible to anyone who may want to view them. If someone e-mails you asking for copies of the handouts that accompanied a presentation you gave at the Medical Library Association, rather than looking for them on the many computers you may use, you can just point them to your online portfolio.

Show and tell

Your cover letter and resume "tells" about your education and experience. The online portfolio "shows" what you've done. When job announcements ask for "evidence of policy development," you can show policies you have written and how they were implemented. Portfolios also allow you to demonstrate your creativity in a way that isn't possible with your cover letter and resume.

Online portfolio tips

Keep it clean and simple.

Make sure it's professional. (Your dog is adorable and we'd love to see your slide show of your last vacation sometime—but a professional online portfolio isn't quite the place.)

Include only materials you'd show colleagues or potential employers.

Use it to add depth to your resume.

Keep it up-to-date (including your contact information).

Make sure it's organized, easy to understand and navigate.

Make sure it's not totally redundant to your cover letter and resume, and that it reflects positively on you.

Many library schools post their students' online portfolio links on their websites. The University of Washington I-School provides links to student online portfolios here:

http://www.ischool.washington.edu/mlis/portfoliosamples.aspx

And you can find examples from The University of Denver here:

https://portfolio.du.edu/pc/index

There are also numerous articles in the library literature and online about online portfolios. LISCareer.com has a number of good articles with excellent tips and step-by-step details for creating good online portfolios, as well as discussing the pitfalls to avoid.

Do you definitely need an online portfolio? Libraries can't function without technology, nor can they function and move forward without technologically savvy librarians. So developing an online portfolio is strongly recommended—but it is worse to have a bad one than not to have one at all. It isn't advisable to try to throw one together overnight.

Getting in the Door

CHAPTER 6

You've finally finished your degree and you're ready to begin job hunting. You need to consider how flexible you are geographically and about the type of position you want. If you cannot move across the country or even across the state, that will narrow the potential job openings. If you aren't tied to any geographical area, you need only focus on getting the type of position you want. If it has always been your dream to get a job in an academic library as a science librarian, you may not want to rule out positions for a science specialist at large public libraries or corporate positions that frequently require technical degrees or experience. However, if it's always been your dream to work with rare books and manuscripts, you will need to look at academic positions, museum-like institutions, large government organization like the Smithsonian and larger public libraries that have special collections, rare books and manuscripts.

Networking

Go to any event held by your school that includes alumni or area librarians. Work it. Print yourself some nice, tasteful business cards. Don't take a stack of resumes and don't give your card out to everyone. Strike up conversations—ask where people work and what they do—and learn as much as possible about different jobs. Ask about openings, and then offer your card. Also give your card to anyone who gives you theirs. The next day, write an e-mail to the librarians that you met, just a simple message saying how much you enjoyed meeting and talking with them. Casual conversations can turn into jobs. Working librarians frequently hear about unadvertised jobs or know about vacancies that are coming up. By networking you may be remembered when a position comes open and your new contacts may let you know about it before it is advertised.

Do the same thing at meetings of the local, state or regional chapters of professional organizations. Get your student chapters to have programs and invite librarians from the area. Go to national conferences of organizations relevant to your job aspirations, like the Public Library Association conference, the American Library Assocation, Special Library Association, the Medical Library Association, the Music Library Association, Law Library Association and so on.

Placement centers

The conferences typically have placement centers. Sign up and bring a sufficient number of resumes, though, in many cases, you'll post your resume online (check the conference placement information before you go). The placement center will list positions, and if there are ones you are interested in you can send a message of interest about the position asking if they have time to interview you at the conference. Employers are viewing your information and may send you a request for an interview on site. You're going to have to be very flexible. You can check back online to see if you have messages but it's very helpful to give your cell phone number to prospective interviewers.

Preliminary interviewing

Many libraries do preliminary interviews at the conferences. It gives you an opportunity to hone your interviewing skills, and it helps prospective employers decide if they want to invite you for an on-site interview. With travel more expensive now, interviews at conferences and telephone interviews have taken on much more importance.

Conferences

Conferences can be costly but can sometimes be as good of an investment as that new interview suit. Most professional associations offer student discounts as well as scholarships to attend annual conferences. If money is tight, which it usually is for students, pool with other students for a hotel room and don't worry much about food. Scour the conference program and the exhibits to find out when and where vendors are hosting breakfasts, luncheons and cocktails. Many vendors have elaborate buffets and open bars to thank their clients or to woo new ones. Breakfasts and luncheons typically involve demonstrations of products but all vendor-sponsored events provide a great opportunity to network.

Finding Jobs

Your library school typically has postings of job openings aimed primarily at entry-level librarians. They may not, however, have all job announcements. The American Library Association's joblist (joblist.ala.org) allows you to post your resume online and communicate with potential employers using the site. You can search and browse position announcements, and set up an RSS feed to receive job postings the minute they are posted.

One of the more comprehensive sources for library and information science job openings is the website LISjobs.com: Jobs for Librarians and Information Professionals. This site lists jobs for academic, public, corporate libraries and other information workplaces. You can search for job openings by state or any keyword—like cataloging or public services. You can also view the daily postings or set up an RSS feed. Lisjobs also posts jobs advertised through library professional associations, such as ALA or the Society of Competitive Intelligence Professionals. For academic librarians, they include job listings from the *Chronicle of Higher Education* and job banks or boards at library schools.

Another good website, Libjobs (www.libjobs.com/index.html) is a job board service provided to corporate, public, academic and K-12 libraries. *Library Job Postings on the Internet,* www.libraryjobpostings.org/moreinfo.htm, is a guide that attempts to link to all library job postings on the internet, including library school placement bulletins and library association job listings. Most of these sites have many other features, including articles related to resumes, job hunting and other advice. You should also check your state library association to see if they have job websites, such as the Illinois Library Association's Job Line (www.ila.org/jobline/index.htm). The source for learning about and applying for federal government positions is USA Jobs at www.usajobs.gov. Other more general sources are Indeed.com and Monster.com, which tend to have positions for corporate libraries that aren't posted elsewhere.

See the appendix of this guide for a full list of job sources.

Placement services

Some library programs have a designated placement service within the school. For example, the University of Texas School of Information Science has a career services office that provides a small career library, a mentoring program, an online job listing board and workshops on resumes and job hunting. Most schools regularly post job openings and offer workshops on how to find jobs. Today, with online job postings, it's not that difficult to find job openings. You can sign up to alerting services through Indeed.com (which picks up all the postings from the University of Texas SIS and those from newspapers and job services) or receive job notices from Lisjobs.com through an RSS feed. Long gone are the days when you had to hang around the student lounge to get your hands on the weekly

Visit Vault at **www.vault.com** for insider company profiles, expert advice, career message boards, expert resume reviews, the Vault Job Board and more.

VAULT CAREER LIBRARY

85

Chronicle of Higher Education, which still posts most academic library positions both in print and online.

The Interview

Your wonderful cover letter and resume landed on the right person's desk (or in their e-mail box) and you are considered for an interview. Many libraries, because of the high cost of travel, are doing their initial interviews by phone.

The phone interview

Most libraries will call or e-mail you to find a mutually convenient time for a telephone interview. If the library is using a search committee, be aware that getting six people together to meet with you may take some juggling. Hopefully the library will have dates and times to propose. Agree to a time and then prepare yourself as you would for an in-person interview (though you don't have to dress up). Take a telephone interview just as seriously as any other type of interview. This may be your one shot to get an on-site interview.

Get organized. You should have already read about the library and the city before you applied for the job, but give yourself a refresher. Hopefully, you've kept a file on each job for which you've applied. Be prepared to answer questions, to talk about your experience, to ask questions— everything that you would in any other interview. In a telephone interview, your audience is getting your voice and your words. Prepare your words, practice speaking with enthusiasm or whatever tone you hope to convey. There is nothing more startling and enlightening than taping yourself in a practice interview and hearing how many times you repeat yourself, say "uh" or that your voice squeaks when you're excited. You don't want to sound like you're taking coffee intravenously but neither do you want to sound like you may doze off any minute. Listen to yourself and practice how you'd like to be heard.

The perils of the phone

This author's first telephone interview was disastrous. She was in the shower when the phone rang. She should have just let it ring, but she grabbed a towel, picked up the phone and discovered that there were five people sitting around a speaker phone on the other end of the line. They had not called in advance to set up the interview. Luckily, she was organized. She had files for each job for which she'd applied, they were in alphabetical order and she'd already written down some questions. She also had a map of the U.S. on my wall by the phone, and had put a different colored pin for each location. The pin also told her how interested she was in each position, and, if nothing else, "where the heck is Edmonton, Oklahoma?" A little obsessive, but if she were applying for a position in Edmonton, Oklahoma, today, she could learn more than she'd want by surfing the web.

On the day of your telephone interview, set yourself up in a quiet comfortable place. Throw the roommate, kid, dog and spouse out. You need quiet so you can hear, so they can hear and so you can think before you respond. Try sitting at your home office desk, or even the dining room table, where you'll have plenty of space to lay out your materials, with a bottle of water. Your audience will most likely be on speaker phone. You may also use a speaker phone so your hands can be free to make notes or look at your materials, but if you do use a speaker phone try your best to be quiet if you need to riffle through your files.

There will be those silences—the dreaded dead air. Do not feel that you need to fill these silences—the search committee may be between questions, taking notes, conferring among themselves or they've accidentally hit the mute button. *Can you hear me now?*

The on-site interview

After all this time and preparation, you get that call that puts a huge smile on your face and makes you want to jump up and down and throw up at the same time. You have a job interview.

Contingencies

The best advice for preparing for an interview is to expect anything to happen. And it can. If you flew in for the interview, your luggage with that nice new interview suit may have gotten lost or delayed. What would you

Visit Vault at **www.vault.com** for insider company profiles, expert advice, career message boards, expert resume reviews, the Vault Job Board and more.

V/\ULT CAREER LIBRARY

87

do? If the library is an hour and a half from the closest airport and someone from the library is supposed to pick you up but doesn't, what will you do? If you forgot to bring the handouts you put together for your presentation, what would you do? If it helps, imagine the worst possible scenario and envision what you would do in that situation. Everyone has their interview nightmare stories.

Hopefully you have taken advantage of any and every interviewing preparation opportunity provided by your school—you've done role playing; you've practiced your presentation; you've practiced answering questions in front of the mirror or employed any other technique that helps you prepare.

Questions to expect

Each library has its own process, but all interviews will involve asking questions. You may meet with several individuals and groups and be asked the same questions over and over. During any breaks, take the opportunity to review some of the questions you've been asked and think of other things you could have added or how you could have answered more articulately. If you can do this, then you'll be able to answer the same questions later with more thought and perhaps a fresh perspective.

This author has been asked such odd questions that she thought she was being interviewed by Barbara Walters—"if you were a tree, what kind of tree would you be?" It seems that there is always an oddball question that may throw you off. That's fine; take your time, then answer as best you can. I think I'm a magnolia tree but I haven't a clue why that would make me a great library director.

You can expect that you will be asked the typical questions:

• What about this position interests you and what makes you uniquely qualified for this position?

• Tell us about yourself.

• What is your ideal working environment?

• Why are you leaving your current position?

• What are your weaknesses?

• What are your strengths?

- If your current supervisor was asked, what would he/she say your strengths and weaknesses are?

- Why did you decide to become a librarian?

- Tell us about your experience working in groups. Can you describe a problem you've had working in a group? How did/would you resolve it?

- What motivates you?

- How well do you manage multiple tasks?

- Do you work well under pressure?

- How do you deal with conflict? Describe a situation where a conflict existed and how you handled it.

- Where do you see yourself in five years?

You'll find that in any type of library job interview, or any job interview for that matter, you will be asked some of the same generic questions. You will also be asked more specific questions related to the position, but first you have to prepare for the typical. Answer the questions honestly. Some will tell you to give the interviewers what they want to hear, but you are cheating yourself and the prospective employers if you don't answer the way you truly feel or think. Do, when possible, be as positive as you can. Everyone hates that question, "what are your weaknesses?" but you have to come up with something—because it will be asked.

Remember that while you are being interviewed for a position, you are also interviewing your prospective boss, co-workers and the organization to see if you even want the job. This author has been on at least two job interviews where the individuals she interviewed with had no clue as to what they were looking for. One was a federal government position and the other was a corporate position. She didn't take either position, because neither had decided how a librarian fit into their organization. Even after a second interview, neither had a clear idea, and as attractive as the salaries and other perks were, it seemed a risk to take either of these positions.

Be prepared

Always bring extra copies of your resume. Use common sense, speak clearly and make eye contact. It's a good idea to bring a pen (maybe two) and a notebook, so you can write down names, notes, questions you want to ask, questions they ask you—especially those three- or four-part

Visit Vault at **www.vault.com** for insider company profiles, expert advice, career message boards, expert resume reviews, the Vault Job Board and more.

V/\ULT CAREER LIBRARY   **89**

questions. There's nothing worse than rambling for five minutes, then asking, "Did I answer your question?"

As a librarian, you shouldn't have to be told to research the organization. Many employers will mail or overnight you a packet ahead of time. Review it and be prepared to answer "what do you know about our library?" Also, review it to prepare your questions for your interviewers. It's the kiss of death when you are asked "What questions do you have for us?" and you don't have any questions.

What to wear

What should you wear? It depends on the type of job, but wearing a suit is always appropriate. A suit is a must for corporate library jobs and upper-level positions in other types of libraries. Wear comfortable shoes—you may be doing a lot of walking. You'll be touring the library, the company, the university, you will be standing if you are asked to make a presentation, you may walk with a group to lunch—you will be on your feet a lot. Interviews are tiring both mentally and physically.

Public Library Interviews

Be prepared for possible interviews by panels of staff, as well as separate interview sessions with groups from various departments. In small public libraries, in addition to interviews with staff, you may also meet with the board of trustees. It is rare that your interview will be one-on-one.

Serving a diverse community

A major difference that separates public libraries from academic or other libraries is that they deal with a much broader range of people—age, economic status, education level and even language. You should be prepared to explain how you'd communicate or offer services for different target groups, such as non-English speakers.

Rather than the research you did as a student, public library patrons ask "everyday"-type questions—how to take care of a hamster, what are the side effects of the medicine a doctor prescribed, prices of used cars, where can I get IRS form 4835 (Farm Rental Income and Expenses), or what's that book everyone is reading about the werewolf ninjas? You need to be prepared to manage being hit with all of those questions in an hour. How would you switch gears? What tools would you use to find this information? If your position will involve helping users choose books to read, review the current *New York Times* bestseller list, make sure you know what Oprah is pushing and be ready to discuss your own reading habits— what is your favorite book? What was the last book you read?

Online research

Learn as much as you can about the library and community it serves. Look at the library website. Look for the community's Chamber of Commerce website, the city/county government's, area economic development websites and tourism websites. Be prepared to answer questions like "what roles does a public library serve in a community?" or "how would you promote the library in the community?" If the library posts its policies and annual reports online, these are excellent sources for learning how the library operates, what its budget is, what its goals are and what its achievements have been.

Some interviews will be formal and some informal. You really won't know until you get there, unless you've spoken with someone who has interviewed at that library before. If you aren't familiar with the role of the board of trustees, do your homework.

The following is one public library's hiring practices and interview process outline.

Hiring practices for the Tuscaloosa Public Library, Tuscaloosa, AL

Key positions

Those typically involved in the interview process are department head, branch head, public relations and youth coordinator. If this is a key position (such as a department head or branch head), the director and HR person usually screen the applications based on the job description and conduct the primary interview.

The process

First, the candidate is given a tour of the library and branches if he requests it. He is given an opportunity to meet with the staff in the department for which he is interviewing. Both department staff and the candidate may ask questions.

Next, other department heads will develop specific questions not covered by the primary interview. Each department head may ask two questions. The candidate may ask any department head questions for about 10 minutes.

Visit Vault at www.vault.com for insider company profiles, expert advice, career message boards, expert resume reviews, the Vault Job Board and more.

VAULT CAREER LIBRARY

91

The department heads provide feedback, with the decision being left to the director as to the best candidate.

Other staff

For branch or department staff, directors of extension services or relevant branch heads are involved in the review process, as is the relevant department head. The library director always is present at the interview.

Once the interviews are over, candidates' strengths and weaknesses are discussed, as are their work history, skills, etc. Usually the director will go with the recommendation of the department head, since she is the one who will be supervising the candidate.

Applicants are ranked; once the HR person checks references, the final candidate is selected.

Provided by Nancy Pack, Director, Tuscaloosa Public Library, Tuscaloosa, Alabama

Academic Library Interviews

Academic libraries typically use a search committee to evaluate candidates, decide whom to interview, develop interview schedules and play a major role in the interview process. The search committee process can be short, but more often it is a lengthy and sometimes painful process for all involved. Interviews for academic library positions can range from half a day to two days with higher level positions extending to three or four days. Academic libraries may ask you to prepare a presentation related to the position. They may give you a topic or they may not. Ask, don't assume, what type of equipment they have. Do you need to bring your laptop? Or is your flash drive all that's needed? It's a good idea to e-mail your presentation to one of your web-based e-mail accounts, just in case your flash drive gets smashed in your bag. Should you make handouts? How many? Who will be your audience for your presentation? Librarians and staff? Faculty and students? Ask.

The following is an example of a large university library's search guidelines. It gives a detailed explanation of the process as well as examples of interview schedules. All libraries don't have as formalized a process as the one below, but if you're interviewing at one that does, this will give you a much better idea of what to expect.

University of Georgia screening/search committee procedure

In colleges, universities, and other institutions of higher education, the selection and appointment of librarians ranks among the most important and consequential decisions to be made. To facilitate these decisions, many library administrators are turning to a consultative arrangement in the selection process. In the University of Georgia Libraries, this process has been formalized by the establishment of a screening/search committee.

Makeup of a search committee

• Supervisor of the vacant position or his/her designee

• Representative from the functional area where the vacancy occurs

• Representative from another functional area in the libraries

• An at-large member whose representation has some application to the vacant position

• Human resources representative

Additional members may be selected as necessary. Where appropriate, members of the classified staff may be appointed to the committee.

Screening and selection process

The screening process, by its nature, takes a great deal of time, especially in searches with large pools of applicants. Everything possible should be done by the screening/search committee to expedite this process to fill the position quickly and to lose as few candidates as possible (e.g., electronic mail, fax, etc.). Each committee establishes its own plan for screening and evaluating nominees and applicants consistent with those established by the university. Whatever procedures are employed, the entire committee is responsible for the legitimacy and timeliness of the process. During the entire screening and selection process, every screening/search committee member and members of the administrative chain for the position (i.e., unit head, assistant head, department head, associate university librarian and university librarian) have full access to the names and complete files of all persons under consideration.

Visit Vault at **www.vault.com** for insider company profiles, expert advice, career message boards, expert resume reviews, the Vault Job Board and more.

VAULT CAREER LIBRARY   93

All candidates, external or internal, are accorded the same treatment in the screening and interview process. Regardless of the level of position, a candidate for any position must provide:

- letter of application/interest

- resume

- names and addresses of at least three references.

Before a candidate for any position can be interviewed, references must be contacted. The committee decides the types of documentation (e.g., resume, letter of application, letters of recommendation, etc.) it will review for each candidate at each stage of the screening process. All candidates must be judged according to the qualifications and requirements stated in the position description and as defined by the screening criteria. The function of the initial screening is to identify and eliminate, early in the search process, applicants who are clearly unqualified. The list of persons who remain under consideration after the initial screening should be those to whom the committee will be giving careful consideration and about whom the committee will be seeking additional information.

Because of interview costs and the prospect of conducting fewer on-site interviews, telephone interviews may be used as an additional method of screening applicants. The telephone interview should be scheduled with the candidate in advance and the entire committee should participate in this conference-call interview. Fair, objective, consistent and equitable processes will be used to narrow the field of candidates to those who are to be invited for interviews.

If, at any time, the committee has further questions regarding a candidate's qualifications or experience, the committee will agree on questions to be asked of the candidates or their references by telephone.

Interviews

All individuals and groups who would interact with the successful candidate should be participants in the interview. If the screening/search committee deems it necessary, a candidate may be required to make a presentation before an appropriate audience. Tours of relevant libraries are strongly encouraged if time permits, but at a minimum, tours should be scheduled for the library (main or science) in which the candidate would be working.

Once the interview schedule is established, it should be put in writing and distributed to all participants in the interview, and announced to the libraries' faculty, and the resumes made available. Whenever possible, the interview schedule will be sent, along with confirmation of the interview date, to the candidate several days prior to the interview. The candidate is also provided with information on the libraries, the university and the town. Changes in the date(s) of a confirmed interview should occur only as a last resort and with notification to all parties concerned.

An interview begins the moment a candidate arrives in town. Members of the search committee should take full advantage of opportunities to spend time with the candidate throughout the interview. Interview responsibilities include:

1. Providing transportation for the candidate from the airport to the hotel.

2. Providing transportation for the candidate from the hotel to the libraries and returning him or her to the hotel, to the airport, or to the airport shuttle after the interview is completed.

3. Arranging dinner the night the candidate arrives with either the department in which the vacancy occurs or with members of the search committee (dinners are reimbursed).

4. Acting as host for the candidate during the interview, i.e., providing guidance and continuity for the candidate, maintaining the timetable and offering a tour of the area.

5. Organizing a lunch group that includes at least one member of the search committee (lunches are reimbursed).

6. Conducting a tour of the libraries.

In most cases, the cost of travel, meals and lodging for external candidates invited to the campus is reimbursed by the libraries. If an off-campus site is selected for the interview, the same financial arrangement should prevail. (There will be no reimbursement for expenses if both the candidate and the libraries' representatives are attendees at a conference.) Candidates are notified in advance of the method of reimbursement. Internal candidates cannot be reimbursed for expenses.

Recommendation of candidate for hire

Any individual or formal group interacting with the candidate should submit a written report to the chair of the screening/search committee by a predetermined date. The chair of the screening/search committee should solicit feedback from persons interacting with the candidate during the

Visit Vault at **www.vault.com** for insider company profiles, expert advice, career message boards, expert resume reviews, the Vault Job Board and more.

V/\ULT CAREER LIBRARY

95

interview process who have not been required to submit a written report (e.g., tour leaders, lunch participants, etc.).

The recommendation of the screening/search committee shall be made in writing and should include a ranked list of all candidates, whether they are acceptable or unacceptable, and how the candidates meet or fail to meet the qualifications specified in the position description. This recommendation should be accompanied by all other written reports. If the administrator disagrees with the recommendation of the screening/search committee, he or she will meet with the committee before taking any action.

The offer

Although final decisions concerning hiring are the responsibility of the university librarian, the department head and/or supervisor are involved in the details surrounding the job offer. Involvement includes both access to information and input into decision-making at each stage of the process.

1. General salary information should be shared with the department head and/or supervisor to facilitate setting the salary for a new hire in the context of other salaries in the department, years of experience, etc.

2. Persons involved in salary negotiations may wish to take the following factors into account: previous professional experience, previous relevant paraprofessional experience of a substantial and highly responsible nature, advanced degrees beyond the MLS; regional salary levels, size of candidate pool, cost and effort of reopening a search vs. acceptability of candidate(s), etc.

3. Copies of the formal letter of offer to the candidate are sent to the supervisor, department head and anyone else in the administrative chain.

The HR or other appropriate administrator is responsible for making the offer. The candidate should be allowed a reasonable period of time, agreed upon by both parties, to reach a decision on the matter.

Announcement of appointment

Upon selection of a candidate and his formal acceptance in writing, the HR representative writes all other active candidates notifying them that the position has been filled. After written acceptance of the position, the appointment is announced.

Extending searches

All active candidates are notified of the intention to extend the search and to readvertise the position should the committee be unable to reach a decision based upon the applications received or should desired qualifications be changed during the search process.

Interview schedule: cataloger

Below is a typical interview schedule for a candidate applying to be a cataloger.

Night before the interview

7:00 p.m.: Have dinner with a small group.

Interview day

8:30 a.m.: Picked up from hotel.

8:45 a.m.: Meeting with the department head.

9:15 a.m.: Tour of the cataloging department and other technical processing areas.

9:45 a.m.: Start the cataloging section heads interview.

10:15 a.m.: Break with members of the cataloging department.

10:45 a.m.: Cataloger's group interview.

11:15 a.m.: Interview with the university librarian.

11:30 a.m.: Lunch.

1:15 p.m.: Take a tour of the library.

1:45 p.m.: Have a meeting with the committee on promotion.

2:15 p.m.: Have the search committee interview.

3:15 p.m.: Benefits review and travel reimbursement information (HR)

3:30 p.m.: Search Progress/Timeline/Questions (HR)

4:00 p.m.: Wrap-up with the department head.

4:15 p.m.: Return to the hotel.

Visit Vault at www.vault.com for insider company profiles, expert advice, career message boards, expert resume reviews, the Vault Job Board and more.

VAULT CAREER LIBRARY   97

Reference/instruction librarian

Here is an interview schedule for a reference/instruction librarian candidate.

Evening before the interview

6:30 p.m.: Dinner with the department head and members of the search committee.

Interview day

7:45 a.m.: Get picked up from the hotel and travel to library.

8:00 a.m.: Get departmental background and mission from the department head.

8:15 a.m.: Take a tour of the department/library with a member of the search committee or department.

8:45 a.m.: Get an overview of the program from the program coordinator.

9:30 a.m.: Candidate presentation.

10:00 a.m.: Have a departmental interview.

10:30 a.m.: Have a coffee break with departmental colleagues.

11:00 a.m.: Travel to other library facilities.

11:15 a.m.: Take a tour of the other library facilities.

11:45 a.m.: Have an interview with the university librarian.

12:00 p.m.: Lunch.

1:15 p.m.: Discussion of benefits and travel reimbursement with human resources staff.

1:30 p.m.: Meet with libraries' faculty committee on promotion.

2:00 p.m.: Break.

2:30 p.m.: Have a brainstorming session with reference colleagues; discuss the impact of Google Scholar on BIs.

3:15 p.m.: Have the search committee interview.

4:00 p.m.: Search progress/timeline (HR).

4:15 p.m.: Wrap up with the department head.

5:00 p.m.: Return to the hotel.

Provided by Florence King, Assistant University Librarian for Human Resources and Director, Student Learning Center Electronic Library, Librarian III.

Other Interview Questions

Below, we list some general questions you might expect to be asked in an interview for any type of library job. All of these are helpful to consider when preparing for your interview. Remember, the best advice for preparing for an interview is to expect anything to happen!

• What work experiences or training have you had that you consider useful preparation for this job?

• Have you worked with an automated library system? If so, what is the name of the system?

• What are some activities that you would do to increase use of the branch library?

• Describe your experience supervising others. What was the largest number of employees that you have supervised? What is the smallest number of employees that you have supervised? What qualities do you look for in a supervisor?

• What is the greatest challenge/problem you have faced with a co-worker? How did you handle the situation? If this happened again, would you do anything differently?

• What experience have you had with selection of materials for collection development? In which subject area(s) do you feel you are most qualified to perform selection?

• How would you handle a complaint from a patron that stated the content of a book was trash and shouldn't be in the library?

• Describe activities that you have performed in the past that have promoted and fostered diversity in collection development and programming.

• What type of programming have you developed? Have you worked with others in the community?

• The WB has a very long-term devoted worker who has served successfully as the branch head for the past several months. "Off the top of your head," without having met this person, can you give us some ideas concerning what you, as branch head, could do to work harmoniously and effectively with this person?

• What type of software have you used? Please describe how you have used it. Have you ever had to troubleshoot minor printer and computer problems?

• Briefly describe how this position fits into your plans for the next several years.

• Describe a project that you have worked on as part of a team. What was your responsibility or role in this project?

• List three of your most important/proudest accomplishments.

• What supervisory experience have you had?

• How would you characterize your supervisory style?

• The person in this position needs to be innovative and proactive. Can you describe some things you have done to demonstrate these qualities?

• How would you rate your communication skills and what have you done to improve them?

• Is there anything other than your school and job experience that qualifies you for this job?

• While this position involves some specific skills (language, computer, cataloging, etc.), it is more of a generalist position. How do you feel your background fits into this?

• Why did you choose X University for your graduate education in library and information science?

• Tell us about X University's online catalog.

• What professional groups are you a member of, and how active have you been in those groups?

• You have just had a short tour of this library. Did any aspect or anything you saw or heard about this library surprise you? Would you change anything about this library?

• Why do you think more students are going into public services than technical services?

• Tell us about your experience with online searching.

- What appeals to you about this position?

- Why do you want to move to this area?

- How do you feel about providing general reference services for undergraduates, or for high school or junior high school students?

- What are some aspects of your present position that you like?

- What are some aspects of your present position that you dislike?

- What do you see yourself doing five or 10 years from now? Or, where do you see yourself going from here?

- What is your cataloging experience?

- What do you think a reference librarian's duties should be?

- Tell us about your subject background and about your course work outside of library science.

- How will your other experiences outside of librarianship aid you in this position?

- What is your opinion of X University's approach to holistic librarianship? How well is the system functioning?

- How are government documents handled at X University?

- What is your interlibrary loan experience?

- What experience have you had using the internet?

- Do you have the skills necessary to create and maintain our WWW home pages?

- What do you see for the future of the internet as a reference tool?

- How will libraries mesh use of print and electronic resources?

- What do you see as the budget implications of increasing use of electronic resources in libraries?

- Can you install software on computers and perform basic maintenance on them?

- What courses (college/graduate school) did you find most satisfying? Least satisfying? Why?

Visit Vault at www.vault.com for insider company profiles, expert advice, career message boards, expert resume reviews, the Vault Job Board and more.

VAULT CAREER LIBRARY 101

- What would you say you learned from your college/graduate school experiences that you see being carried over to your life today?

- Do you plan to continue your education?

- What kind of people do you like to work with?

- What kind of people do you find it most difficult to work with? What do you do to improve the situation?

- Do you prefer working alone or in groups?

- Starting with your last job, would you tell me about some of your achievements that were recognized by your superiors?

- What are some things you would like to avoid in a job? Why?

- What are some of the things for your jobs that you feel you have done particularly well?

- What does success mean to you? How do you judge it?

- What are some of the things about your last job that you found difficult to do?

- What are some of the problems you encounter in doing your job? Which one frustrates you the most? What do you usually do about it?

- How has your present job developed you to take on even greater responsibilities?

- Who or what in your life would you say influenced you most with regard to your career objectives?

- What traits or qualities do you feel could be strengthened or improved?

- What kinds of things do you feel most confident in doing? Somewhat less confident in doing?

- What are some of the thing you are either doing now or have thought about doing that are self-development activities?

- Tell me about a time when you had work problems or stresses that were difficult for you.

- Customers frequently create a great deal of pressure. What has been your experience in this area?

- What types of pressures do you experience on your current job? How do you cope with these pressures?

- Describe a time when you were under pressure to make a decision. Did you react immediately or take time in deciding what to do?

- What types of things make you angry? How do you react?

- How do you react when you see co-workers disagreeing? Do you become involved or hold back?

- Do you prefer to have a job in which you have well laid-out tasks and responsibilities, or one in which your work changes on a frequent basis?

- In your current position, what types of decisions do you make without consulting your immediate supervisor?

- What types of experiences have you had in dealing with difficult customers?

- Describe a problem person you have had to deal with. What did you say or do?

- What has been your experience in dealing with the general public? When have people really tried your patience?

- What important goals have you set in the past, and how successful have you been in working toward their accomplishment?

- Do you do personal planning? If so, what are your goals?

- What things give you the greatest satisfaction?

- How would you describe yourself?

- In what ways do you think you can make a contribution to our department?

- What two or three accomplishments have given you the most satisfaction? Why?

- Describe your most rewarding experience.

- What do you know about our library? University? Community? Company?

- If you were hiring someone for this job, what qualities would you look for?

- How do you feel about your ability to write, spell and communicate? What kind of feedback have you received about your writing ability?

- Describe your experience in creating documents, proposals, research findings or any other form of written copy.

Visit Vault at **www.vault.com** for insider company profiles, expert advice, career message boards, expert resume reviews, the Vault Job Board and more.

VAULT CAREER LIBRARY   **103**

- What does the term two-way communication mean to you? When have you successfully used two-way communication?

- Some people get to know strangers quickly, while others prefer to take their time letting people get to know them. Describe how you entered relationships when you were "new" on a job.

- Some people have the ability to "step into another's shoes." When has this skill been required of you?

- How did you organize your work in your last position? What happened to your plan when emergencies came up?

- Describe how you determined your priorities on your last job.

- Describe how you schedule your time on an unusually hectic day. Give a specific example.

- Are you a person who likes to "try new things," or "stay with regular routines"? Give an example.

- What is your philosophy of reference?

- What are your three (or five) favorite reference books? Or, if you were on a desert island, which three or five reference books would you want to have?

If you're interviewing for positions at academic libraries, consider the following questions.

- What would you do about implementing the provisions of the American with Disabilities Act (or some other new policy) in our library, and how would you prioritize this among your other duties?

- What do you feel is the place of instruction in the library? Have you ever taught in a classroom setting? Would you be comfortable teaching library use workshops or courses?

- What experience do you have dealing with academic scholars?

After the Interview

If you do nothing else after interviewing with a library or organization, you must send a thank-you note to the individuals who interviewed you. Today, e-mail is acceptable, as well as timely and convenient. Try to e-mail everyone you met with during the interview. A well-written e-mail that is personalized to each individual reinforces your performance during the interview. If it isn't possible to e-mail everyone, be sure to e-mail the library director and the direct supervisor for the position for which you interviewed. Don't have their e-mail addresses? Check their website for a staff directory.

Awaiting a decision

The search process can be short but, depending on any imaginable thing that could arise, searches can extend from months to a year. Libraries of different types typically have their own schedule. Their search process may be formal and standardized, or more informal or flexible depending on the position. Interviews for entry-level positions can range from half a day to two days, with higher-level positions extending to three or four days.

Once you have interviewed, you should have some idea of the search process. Typically the personnel director or person in charge of the interview will give you an indication of how many people are interviewing and when the organization hopes to make its decision. Of course, searches that are done by search committees can take longer than if only one or two individuals is responsible for the hiring. If you were the first of three to be interviewed, then the dates of the other interviews—whether they're the same week or spread across a number of weeks—can give you an indication of how long you may have to wait. Bringing in candidates from out of town typically requires more time due to the need for travel arrangements and to make sure that all search committee members and other decision-makers can be available on interview dates.

Regardless of the type of library position, before you leave the interview, ask the personnel librarian or officer when he hopes to make a decision. Not every library has a personnel librarian, so ask the most appropriate person depending on the library—it may be the chair of a search committee, the library director, the department head or president of the library board.

Visit Vault at www.vault.com for insider company profiles, expert advice, career message boards, expert resume reviews, the Vault Job Board and more.

VAULT CAREER LIBRARY   105

The offer and negotiation

Typically, the personnel director/librarian, library director or other manager within the organization will call when you are being offered the position. The offer should include the salary and proposed starting date. You are not expected to accept a position on the spot but neither should you be unreasonable in asking for more than a week to decide unless there are extenuating circumstances. Remember that other candidates may have been interviewed and the library may have a second choice should you not accept. The library will not notify the others interviewed until they have a firm acceptance from you. Consider that you were in candidate No. 2's position and were left waiting another week to learn the outcome of the job search.

What if you never hear from the library? Should you contact the library if you haven't heard from it within the time frame that it planned to make a decision? Most people won't mind if applicants e-mail or call concerning the status of a search. At the same time, employers don't want to be pestered every day by the same individual.

CAREERS

ON THE JOB

LIBRARY
CAREERS

Careers Paths and Lifestyle

CHAPTER 7

Career Paths

Within both academic and public libraries there are many positions ranging from acquisitions (librarians and staff who order books), to electronic resources librarians who review databases and other online resources for purchase or licensing, to cataloging librarians who catalog and process the materials once they arrive and assure that there are records in the library's online catalog for each item, to special collections librarians who work with rare documents or books, develop archival plans for their library or develop digital collection of rare materials. Within each type of library there are many other types of positions.

There truly isn't a typical career path for librarians, but to get an increase in salary one typically needs to advance within their current organization or move to another library. Raises within academic and public libraries can be slow—frequently under 5 percent a year with an occasional year when salaries are frozen and there are no increases. Some libraries are on a pay grade system or a promotional system; when a librarian is promoted from Librarian I to Librarian II or from Assistant Professor to Associate Professor, there may be a bump in salary in addition to an annual raise.

A librarian staying in the same organization typically receives annual raises based on performance. After three to five years of experience, should a department head position open up, one would need to apply for that position either through an internal search process or a national search process.

Academic library path

In an academic library, a typical career path might be librarian, followed by coordinator (a non-supervisory position—for example, within a reference or information services department, coordinating a specific function such as instruction or electronic resources). The next move up would be department head. For example, a collection development librarian might move up to head of the collection development department, supervising librarians and support staff in the department. The next step up after department head might be assistant director for public services, technical services or another main function of the library. An assistant director for public services would oversee the access services department (or circulation, as it's known in many libraries), interlibrary loans, reference or information services, government information, media services and other departments that deal primarily with the public. If the library is large enough, there may be another layer of management, such as associate director, or perhaps a special unit headed by a position like director of innovative technologies. Ultimately the highest position within an academic library would be library director, dean of libraries or university librarian, positions paying $80,000 to well over $100,000 depending on the library's size.

Public library path

The career path within a public library is similar. The next step for an assistant adult services librarian could be a management position, in this case head of the adult services department. Depending on the size of the library, the next step up would be deputy director, then library director. If a library has a central library in addition to branch locations, a librarian may move from a department head to branch manager. A large public library may have many departments, including administration, archives, audiovisual, business information, cataloging and acquisition, computer learning, fine arts, foreign literature, general reference, government reference, history and geography, library services for the blind, literature, readers advisory, science and technology, systems (which would include electronic resources, the online catalog and circulation system and web applications), special collections and youth Services. Department head and branch manager positions in larger public libraries pay between $50,000 and $90,000, while a deputy county librarian for a large library system may pay in the range of $115,000 to $150,000.

Those able to be mobile geographically may move from institution to institution to better their salary. As with many jobs, two to five years' experience can make a difference in salary when making a move. Some librarians may spend their entire career at the same library, but it is often easier to move up by moving around.

Moving between library types

Can librarians move between different types of libraries with ease? It depends on the position, and having a subject specialty can help. A business librarian may find it easy to move from an academic library to a corporate library or a large public library that has a business information services department. Corporate business librarians may easily adapt to an academic library. On the other hand, a public library business specialist may be able to move into an academic or corporate library, but the move may not be as easy—it depends greatly on the size of the public library and the education, skills and experience of the candidate. Having an undergraduate degree in business helps, and some academic and corporate librarians may prefer librarians who have an MBA in addition to their MLIS. Other subject specialists who may be able to move easily between types of libraries are those with strong medical, science and technology backgrounds. Because there is a shortage of catalogers today, librarians in those positions should have no trouble moving between types of libraries.

The Reference Desk

This author has been fortunate to work in many different libraries and environments. The majority of her career has been spent in a public services or management position in an academic library, but two of those positions were in a business academic library and the other in a health sciences library. She also worked for a government agency library in an administrative position and currently is director of a small public library.

She began her career as a reference librarian in an academic library. For the next eight years, she worked in two different academic libraries. But the work consisted, and still consists to some extent, of working the reference or information desk. At this desk, she would assist students and faculty in finding materials and information to answer their questions for their assignments or research. The traffic at the reference desk has declined over the years due to the library's purchasing of online databases, full-text journals and magazines and the overall familiarity of most students in using the Web. But the reference desk remained a busy place through the mid-1990s, and at one large university library where she worked, frequently three librarians worked at the desk at the same time. Today, many librarians complain of sitting at the desk and waiting for questions. As a result, the model of reference service has changed drastically in the last 15 years.

Reference today

Today a reference or information services librarian in an academic library may answer questions or guide a student's research by e-mail or "virtual" reference. Virtual references are services using a system like OCLC's Questionpoint or other software where reference librarians answer questions using "live" chat and co-browsing databases or web sites with the user. These services are typically available 24 hours a day, seven days a week, staffed by a cooperative of librarians throughout the country serving their own patrons or another academic library's students and faculty. Additionally, Questionpoint "back-up" librarians augment library staff during busy times, holidays and the overnight hours. Students today are accustomed to IMing and chat through online services such as Yahoo!, AOL, MSN and Google, so it's sometimes more natural for the students than for the librarians.

Academic reference

Reference librarians in academic libraries fill the rest of their day with staff meetings, committee meetings and collection development, which involves purchasing books and other materials to serve the needs of their library users. Reference librarians also develop guides to research in particular subjects that have high demand—topics like "How to research a company," how to find articles on a particular topic or how to use specific databases. Typically, these guides are available online, posted on the library websites, on websites for particular classes or within the online reserve (required reading) resources a professor has placed on "reserve" for a specific class.

User education

Reference librarians also spend a lot of time on user education. Again, some of this comes in the form of tutorials and guides developed by librarians and placed online, while the majority of this instruction takes place in the classroom. Universities may require library orientation or information literacy classes for all incoming freshmen; libraries may offer specific workshops aimed at a broad audience, such as career research or term paper research; or librarians, at the request of faculty, may guest lecture in classes to instruct and inform students about resources available that are specific to their assignments.

Public reference

Reference librarians in public libraries also assist individuals in finding information, though they serve all ages and cover all subjects. In the largest public libraries, reference librarians may work only in children's and young adult services, in adult services or in specialized areas, such as business and science. Questions in public libraries range from "how to start a small business" to information on medications a person has been prescribed to helping students in high school and younger with homework assignments.

Reference librarians, or public service librarians as they are called in many libraries, arrange workshops, teach beginning computer classes, give tours to school children and sponsor events intended to get people into the library. Librarians in public libraries frequently work on grant proposals, marketing and promotion of their library and its services, and sometimes write a column for their town or city's newspaper.

Young Adult services

A young adult services librarian in a public library might form a teen advisory group to advise him or her about their information needs, or hold video gaming nights and tie those into related books. The librarian also plans for special events, such as National Teen Reading Week or Banned Books Week, and designs exhibits and displays related to Black History Month, financing college and other topics of interest to teens. Many librarians start blogs to inform their library audience of new resources, or so that their teens can submit book reviews and information they have found helpful in their homework. Librarians may also develop MySpace and Facebook pages to reach out to their library users.

Children's services

A children's services librarian in a public library does similar work as a young adult services librarian, but she serves a different audience. A children's services librarian plans summer reading programs, story hours, goes out to speak or read to pre-k and kindergarten classes, and promotes reading and learning among young children.

Hours

Reference librarians in both academic and public libraries frequently work nights and weekends. They may work one night a week and one weekend a month, or they may work hours that the library isn't normally open to present workshops or hold events.

Salaries

Salaries span a wide range depending on the type of library, the type of position and the geographic region where the library is located. The 2008 edition of *ALA-APA Salary Survey: Librarian—Public and Academic* shows that the mean salary for librarians with ALA accredited master's degrees reported an increase of 2 percent from 2007, up $1,151 to $57,809. The

Visit Vault at www.vault.com for insider company profiles, expert advice, career message boards, expert resume reviews, the Vault Job Board and more.

VAULT CAREER LIBRARY   113

median ALA MLS salary was $53,251 and salaries ranged from $22,000 to $331,200. Some state library associations have set minimum salaries; however, these are only guidelines and some are based on a formula which might include the comparable salary for public school teachers in the community. The North Atlantic Region of the country has the highest salaries overall, followed by the West Coast, then the Midwest and finally the South. These are overall tendencies and within each library type and region of the country there are always exceptions.

Library living wage

The ALA-APA Council passed a living wage resolution for library employees at the American Library Association meeting in Anaheim, California in 2008. It adopted a resolution entitled "Endorsement of a Nonbinding Minimum Salary for Professional Librarians," resulting in a nonbinding endorsement of a "minimum salary for professional librarians of not less than $40,000 per year." Adjusted for inflation, this amounts to $41,680.

The salary committee was also charged "to guide ALA-APA activities in support of better salaries, comparable worth, pay equity, and similar programs related to the status of librarians and other library workers." The committee identified the need to strengthen ALA-APA's position with regard to wages and salaries for all library employees, and with regard to variable costs of living over time and across geographical locations.

Federal government and special libraries tend to pay more to start and continue to provide healthy increases based on performance and moving up within the organization. Academic entry-level librarian salaries begin as low as the mid-30s and sometimes creep into the mid-40s, but once in a position salary increases may be slow unless one moves into an administrative role. Public library salaries can be even lower to start, and public library salaries tend to be lower overall except in the largest public libraries.

Administrative salaries are considerably higher. A director of a large public library system might over $100,000, as can a dean of libraries or university librarian.

The following table presents selected position with salaries for Public and Academic Library Jobs.

Selected salaries for public and academic libraries

Position	Size	Type	Min	Medium	Max
Librarians who do not supervise	Small	Public	$22,000	$39,392	$52,241
	Very Large	Public	$23,310	$47,299	$84,453
	Four-year	Academic	$27,800	$44,000	$70,455
	University	Academic	$25,952	$48,000	$91,140
Collection Development	Small	Public	$24,960	$27,000	$52,241
	Large	Public	$23,728	$35,482	$84,453
	Four-year	Academic	$27,198	$37,257	$70,455
	University	Academic	$21,238	$48,000	$91,140
Children's Servies	Small	Public	$13,455	$28,664	$56,160
	Very Large	Public	$23,130	$37,063	$60,707
Librarian Manager	Small	Public	$26,998	$42,016	$74,352
	Very Large	Public	$33,550	$48,449	$108,400
	University	Academic	$29,000	$50,670	$99,443
Webmaster	Very Large	Public	$38,834	$54,835	$69,576
	University	Academic	$21,074	$43,255	$69,576

Source: American Library Association–Allied Professional Association Survey (ALA/APA), 2008

Keep in mind that these aren't starting salaries and they are ranges for the entire country. Different regions of the country may have higher or lower salaries and as the table shows, salaries can vary greatly by type and size of library.

Special library salaries

Special and corporate library salaries can start considerably higher and tend to be higher overall. In the *2008 Special Library Association Salary Survey*, the average salary was reported to be $71,812. The following table presents the ranges of salaries. The salaries presented are for the U.S.,

Visit Vault at **www.vault.com** for insider company profiles, expert advice, career message boards, expert resume reviews, the Vault Job Board and more.

VAULT CAREER LIBRARY **115**

though the survey includes salaries for Canada, the United Kingdom and Europe.

10th Percentile	Median	Mean	90th Percentile
$42,000	$66,000	$71,812	$108,000

Source: 2008 SLA Salary Survey

Government library salaries

Federal government library salaries are based upon the General Schedule (below) set by the U.S. Office of Personnel Management. Most federal library positions began at Grade 9, though there are other federal wage systems used by the Department of Defense.

SALARY TABLE 2009-GS

EFFECTIVE JANUARY 2009

Annual Rates by Grade and Step

Grade	Step 1	Step 2	Step 3	Step 4	Step 5	Step 6	Step 7	Step 8	Step 9	Step 10	W/in Grade Amounts
9	$40,949	$42,314	$43,679	$45,044	$46,409	$47,774	$49,139	$50,504	$51,869	$53,234	$1,365
10	$45,095	$46,598	$48,101	$49,604	$51,107	$52,610	$54,113	$55,616	$57,119	$58,622	$1,503
11	$49,544	$51,195	$52,846	$54,497	$56,148	$57,799	$59,450	$61,101	$62,752	$64,403	$1,651
12	$59,383	$61,362	$63,341	$65,320	$67,299	$69,278	$71,257	$73,236	$75,215	$77,194	$1,979
13	$70,615	$72,969	$75,323	$77,677	$80,031	$82,385	$84,739	$87,093	$89,447	$91,801	$2,354
14	$83,445	$86,227	$89,009	$91,791	$94,573	$97,355	$100,137	$102,919	$105,701	$108,483	$2,782
15	$98,156	$101,428	$104,700	$107,972	$111,244	$114,516	$117,788	$121,060	$124,332	$127,604	$3,272

Source: Office of Personnel Management

Federal librarian salaries may also be adjusted from the above GS system based upon geographic region. In addition to the salaries listed for each grade and step level, some librarians receive additional locality pay. For example, a federal position in Atlanta salary would be higher than a federal job in a rural area. The salary of $48,545 for a GS-9 Step 1 in Atlanta is $48,545 opposed to $40,949 in the country.

Uppers and Downers

Perks galore

There are some perks to librarian positions, regardless of the type of library. Those with a curiosity for learning and finding answers will find the work satisfying. Readers and book lovers can still find their place as long as they keep in check that libraries aren't just about books—information is the game. To some, getting the first look at the books coming in, or better yet an advance copy, is a big perk. Most librarians find the unending opportunities to learn, formally and informally, to be a perk. The variety that comes with a job at most libraries is a major benefit; it's hardly likely that any two days will be the same. Flexible schedules are allowed at some organizations so a typical 9 to 5 isn't always the case. Working that monthly or quarterly weekend doesn't seem so bad when you exchange that for two days off during the week, and if you're a night owl there are jobs where you may work all nights or a few nights a week. There are also jobs that allow librarians to work at home.

Helping people

It sounds corny (and some librarians cringe at this) but people who like people will enjoy working in public services departments of libraries. Librarianship is considered by many a "helping" profession. Whether a student working on a term paper, a faculty member compiling data, a sixth-grade class researching different countries while learning library research methods, a senior citizen looking for information on prescriptions or alternative treatments, a young mother looking for parenting books, an entrepreneur seeking information to assist in developing a business plan or a person wanting information on learning a software program like Adobe Photoshop, librarians help people find information. Librarians may not be thanked in the acknowledgments of someone's book (though they frequently are) or with an award from patrons or students, but the thanks

Visit Vault at **www.vault.com** for insider company profiles, expert advice, career message boards, expert resume reviews, the Vault Job Board and more.

VAULT CAREER LIBRARY   **117**

do come. They may come in the form of a picture drawn by second-graders who visited the library, applause at the end of a lecture to a college class on finding information for their assignments, fresh produce from a senior who took a computer class, a MBA student who buys the entire library staff pizza at the end of the term or the homemade cookies or candy made by one of the library's board members. These are little things, but they are appreciated.

Feeding the intellect

For many academic librarians, the chance to stay in a college/university environment is its own reward. For those who require intellectual stimulation, an academic library and its parent organization may provide an intellectual and sometimes cultural oasis in even the smallest college town. As faculty or staff at a university, librarians may also receive as a benefit free tuition for themselves, their spouse and/or children. This author has known a number of academic librarians who have stayed in their current positions until their children have completed their college degrees.

Benefits

Librarians at all types of libraries may be given financial support and time off to attend continuing education workshops and to attend conferences. Most libraries offer excellent health insurance plans to their full-time employees, with some offering matching contributions to retirement plans, ample vacation time and holidays and travel budgets. Rather than one week of vacation when starting another job, librarians may accrue a day or more a month.

Compared to other careers these perks may seem meager. Librarians don't get a company car, an expense account or large year-end bonuses (unless you count the turkey at Christmas). But for many, being able to work in a field that they love is enough.

Lagging salaries

If asked about the biggest downer of the job, most librarians would probably say salary. Entry-level librarians are now making between $38,000 and $42,000 in large academic and public libraries. To many, that doesn't seem enough for a person who has a master's degree. Raises are slow to come, and some years a raise may not come at all.

Job hunting

Otherwise, one of the biggest downers among some newly minted MLS graduates is the difficulty in finding a job. For several years grant and scholarship money has been healthy enough to attract new individuals to the professions, and reports from the government and the American Library Association have trumpeted a high availability of positions—even a shortage of librarians. And the Bureau of Labor Statistics reports, "despite slower-than-average projected employment growth, job opportunities are still expected to be favorable because a large number of librarians are expected to retire in the coming decade." The retirement prediction may be true, but the reality may be that positions vacated by librarians are at the management level; that many entry-level positions are being filled by non-professionals or those with degrees in information technology or computer science; or because of tight budgets, positions vacated by people retiring may be combined and/or eliminated.

Budget cuts

A major downer for all types of libraries is budget cuts. Early ways of dealing with budget cuts are reducing hours, putting renovations on hold and/or spending less on resources, but in worst case scenarios some public library systems have been forced to close branch libraries while other systems face complete closure. In 2007 in Southern Oregon, the website of the Jackson County Libraries (15 in all) posted the following notice: "All 15 Jackson County Library Branches WILL BE CLOSED as of Saturday, April 7, 2007, due to a lack of funding." The libraries in this rural area of Oregon lost $7 million in federal funding from timber subsidy payments. After the closures, voters rejected a property tax levy to fund reopening the libraries. The libraries eventually reopened anyway, but the county outsourced the running of the libraries to the Germantown, Maryland company Library Systems and Services. Many former employees were able to return to their jobs, but staff and hours overall were cut. Other libraries in Oregon and in other states have faced similar problems and have turned to friends' groups for fund raising. More recently, the Mayor of Philadelphia announced the closing of 11 libraries on January 1, 2009. City Council members fought this, taking the mayor to court, and many parents and city workers launched a lawsuit. As of this writing, a judge has ruled that the mayor doesn't have the authority to close the libraries, but the city still faces a $1 billion budget deficit.

Library cuts and closings aren't only the problem of public libraries. In 2006, the closing of many of the EPA (Environmental Protection Agency) libraries were part of former President Bush's cost-cutting plan that included a proposed reduction of $100 million for FY 2007 and further cuts for FY 2008. In fall 2008, three regional libraries and the central library reopened, after Congressional hearings and a General Accounting Office report.

One major result of budget-trimming at many libraries is an increasing number of part-time librarians. The salaries for these part-time positions may be comparable to full time, but part-time librarians don't earn benefits—thus the parent organization is saving on insurance, vacation and sick leave, pay for holidays, retirement contributions and any other monetary benefits a full-time librarian or other full-time employee would receive. More and more new and experienced librarians are finding that they may need to cobble together two or three jobs to not only make a full-time salary but to have the money to pay their own health insurance.

Other annoyances

Other downers? Sure, there are other things to complain about. Parents drop their kids off for the librarians to babysit; college students can't search Google, much less library databases; cell phones constantly ring despite posted signs against their use in the library; some public librarians find that the only books people want to read are the best sellers, occasional library patrons still think some books should be banned (including *The Adventures of Tom Sawyer*); complaints that with public computers and wi-fi internet access, libraries are promoting pornography; and the perception among some of the general public that people can find all of the information they need on the internet. Most dramatically, librarians sometimes are the last defense between you and the FBI—in one instance, two agents appeared and asked a public library to turn over the names of library patrons who had read books on Osama Bin Laden.

Career Changers

Many who enter the profession are career changers. This author received her undergraduate degree in business and worked in publishing and finance before she decided she wanted to do something different. What made her decide? She knew she wanted to do something different but didn't quite know what that was yet. Part of her job at the time was to research companies. One day she was in a university library doing research on companies that might be prospective clients when she looked up and around at her surroundings and realized how much she was enjoying this afternoon of research. She thought "I wonder how you get a job in a place like this?" She knew she'd have to go back to school but she thought it would be to complete another four-year undergraduate degree. She went to the reference desk and asked the librarian. He quickly found several reference books for her that gave her information about education requirements, different graduate programs as well as other information she needed to know—like she needed to register right away to take the GRE (Graduate Record Exam). She was quite excited to know that the MLIS degree was a one- or two-year degree depending on where you went to school. To think that she could embark on a new career that quickly was very exciting. She'd never worked in a library but she'd spent a lot of time in them growing up, in college and in her job. She put herself on the fast track and registered to take the GRE as soon as possible, began filling out applications to different programs, and found herself enrolled in a program in only seven months. She also landed one of the graduate library assistant positions in the university library where she was getting her degree.

Other career changers may be people who pursued other degrees, then discovered the work wasn't as they envisioned; or they got PhDs but never found the right tenure-track position teaching at a university; or others who worked for 20 years in their first career and then turned to librarianship as their second career. In a recent article in *Library Journal*, a survey listed some of the former careers of recent MLIS graduates. The largest portion had previously worked in some area of education, followed by business, social work and human service, and healthcare. Many people entering MLIS programs have worked in bookstores, museums, computer science and publishing, writing and editing. Regardless of the program and school that one chooses, his class will be made up of individuals from diverse backgrounds educationally and in their former professions.

My career change experience

I became a librarian for a lot of the usual idealistic reasons, along with feeling that I needed a new career during the housing/building bust/recession of the early 1980s. I can't say that I stumbled into it. If there is a librarian gene, I have it. My mom and her mom were both librarians. So I got some encouragement there. Additionally, my body was telling me that it didn't like my job as a carpenter/laborer for a builder.

Visit Vault at **www.vault.com** for insider company profiles, expert advice, career message boards, expert resume reviews, the Vault Job Board and more.

V/\ULT CAREER LIBRARY   **121**

I already had an undergraduate degree in anthropology but I started back to school, part-time, with the idea of getting a degree in secondary education so I could teach science. After I figured out that it would take five years going full-time, and that essentially none of my undergraduate courses would count toward my new degree, I looked around and applied to library school. I thought, idealistically, that I could still fill a "teaching" role by being a reference librarian in a public library, and thus follow in my mom's and grandmother's footsteps.

I had worked in a library before. As an undergraduate at Southern Illinois University in Carbondale, I worked in the Social Studies library (floor) of the main library, but it really didn't influence my decision.

I'm working part-time for the U. S. Forest Service libraries, doing retrospective conversion cataloging of their old documents. I think what makes me a good cataloger is that I'm interested in just about any subject matter, so I don't get bored. My skill is in solving the bibliographical puzzles that are presented to me.

Bill Paine
Part-time cataloger, U.S. Forest Service

In my late 40s, I had to admit that my position as a vice president, client services for a software development company just wasn't all that satisfying. I was working long hours for reasonable rewards, but there was always the risk of a company downsizing.

A friend told me about the master's in library science program at the University of Kentucky. It intrigued me. I speculated on transitioning from customer service into corporate competitive intelligence. My sister offered to put me up at her house so that I could "power through" the program in six semesters. Toward the end of the program, I opted to try an academic library internship in the reference group of the University of Louisville Library. It changed everything. It was fun and challenging, and I loved working with the students and faculty.

When I finished my degree, I started interviewing for business library positions, and settled at the Kopolow Business Library at Washington University in St. Louis. Almost three years later, I couldn't be happier. Academic libraries are reinventing themselves to ride a tidal wave of information technology, and there's a need for independent eyes to help manage the changes. The work I'm involved in is broad in scope and constantly changing. Any week, I might be giving the executive MBA class an overview of resources, figuring out how to justify the cost of a research database or designing usability tests for our website. Because of my business experience, I was able to hit the ground running.

When you're making a career change, it's not always easy to predict how it will go. I've given up some serious earning power in order to strike out in a new direction. It's been wobbly a few times at the beginning, when I was sorting out the cultural differences. Librarians, like most academicians, are collegial and collaborative. Decisions are made by committee, and everything takes much longer than you could justify in the business world. I'm learning patience and flexibility.

It also takes humility if you're are stepping down in order to change career paths. If you take advantage of the "down-time" to really learn, you'll be ready to advance again. Of course, you may just enjoy the respite. I'm glad I've got a career now that allows me to grow each day, and contribute with gusto, and then go home to friends and family. Who could ask for more?

Carol Mollman
Business Librarian
Washington University

As you can tell, there's no such thing as a typical librarian.

Visit Vault at **www.vault.com** for insider company profiles, expert advice, career message boards, expert resume reviews, the Vault Job Board and more.

VAULT CAREER LIBRARY   123

Librarian Profiles

CHAPTER 8

Academic Library: Web Services Coordinator

In *The Accidental Systems Librarian*, Rachel Singer Gordon deftly captures how someone who might be a bit more technologically savvy than the average person, or even someone who shows interest in troubleshooting technology, can "accidentally fall" into a systems librarian type of position. She describes what a systems librarian might encounter and essential skills to develop. Since I graduated from library school, my interest in web services and improving a library's virtual presence has increased, so many technology responsibilities have fallen in my lap because of my aptitude and curiosity.

It was not my original intent to become a systems librarian. My last two jobs were split positions, and there can be benefits as well as challenges to this. Often in a small or branch library, a techie's role can be split between several areas: reference, instruction, collection development, being a departmental liaison, electronic resources, desktop support, server maintenance and web page management. While I gained experience in many areas within a library and became well rounded, my technological skills were degrading from not being in an environment that focused on the development of technological projects. I was the sole person on the technology team. Now I am in a web services department of a large academic library where my job encompasses dealing with the back-end of systems, installing and managing open-source tools like wikis and blogs, and working with our library's federated search tool, content management system, digital library asset management tool, and other tools that enable and support communication and collaboration. The coolest part about my job is that I am always learning what new technologies are just down the street and I get to "play" with them to see if they might enhance our workflow or our online services.

Rachel Vacek, University of Houston Libraries

Public Library Director

There is no such thing as a typical day as director of a small city library. There's also no such thing as a day going as you planned it. Just think of all the details of every job in the library and some aspect of each of them winds up on the director's desk. In terms of collection development, after hundreds of years, we seem to have the "book" thing down pretty well, but technology keeps changing every other aspect. Take audiobooks—how long do we keep the cassette collection? Are we going to start buying MP3 CDs as well as the "old" format? And what about Playaways? How (and where!) are we going to shelve all these different formats? Are we going to buy the same title in downloadable form as well? How are we going to divvy up the budget to cover all of this, and with what proportion going to which? Repeat this conversation with the reference department, just substituting print periodicals and reference books vs. databases and microforms. And repeat it again as soon as another new format, or another budget year comes along.

There are also decisions—and crises—with the physical plant. In Beverly, like many libraries, we are having problems with our HVAC. I get to deal with staff and patron complaints at the same time as I am trying to coordinate with all the layers of other city departments and contractors to fix the thing—and to struggle with where the money is going to come from. In the meantime, there are meetings and lots of e-mails regarding doing the landscaping at our branch—something that wasn't done when a new addition was added because we didn't have the money at that time. I've also got meetings to plan and attend regarding the fund raising we are doing for a new Bookmobile. Beverly has provided bookmobile service to our schools, senior living centers and neighborhoods since 1952, and our current bookmobile accounts for 18 percent of our total circulation—nearly 60,000 items a year. It is also 21 years old and literally losing parts on the road. Somewhere in my day I am supposed to be researching and writing a couple of grants for the Bookmobile, as well as pushing forward the local campaign, with organizing fund raisers and letters to local businesses, etc. Of course, in the middle of this I get a call that a sinkhole has developed in the parking lot—that definitely wasn't on my list of "to do's" for the day!

Up on the roof

Budgets, reports, meetings with the other directors in our consortia, meetings with my department heads, participating in material selection, planning and doing programming, filling in on the desk (we're always a bit short-staffed!), meeting with reporters and with city councilors and with trustees, talking to patrons and climbing out on the roof to check on the leaking skylight—there's never a dull moment. It can be frustrating trying to stay on top of so many diverse aspects of the job at the same time, not to mention learning so many things that were never taught in library school (HVAC 101 anyone?), but I enjoy it. And sometimes, just sometimes, I get to plan ahead for where the library is going to be five, or even 10 years down the road!

Pat Cirone, Beverly Public Library, Beverly, Mass.

Contract Librarian

I am a professional librarian who works from home. After years of working as a reference librarian and library instruction coordinator in academic libraries, a director of a special library and a reference manager of a large public library, I now own my own business. I am an independent contractor with a major library organization and currently work answering reference questions online serving libraries across the United States and the United Kingdom.

No two days have the same schedule. Each is different, and I like that. As many busy professionals, I keep my schedule handy and check it often. I post a calendar of my work schedule outside the door of the computer room so my family knows my schedule and can guess when they might see their next meal or be able to get to the PC for homework.

Shifting shifts

During most of the year, I work 25 to 30 hours a week on this contract. I tend to work two to three shifts a day, generally each shift lasting two hours each. It might be 10 a.m. to noon and 9 to 11 p.m. one day; 2 to 4 p.m., 6 to 8 p.m., 7 to 9 p.m. another. There seem to be endless combinations.

In between those shifts I run errands, prepare meals, attend appointments and meetings, exercise, tend to relatives in need, help with the household chores and participate in family activities. I stay current on what is happening in libraries by talking with other professionals, reading and looking at library websites.

Visit Vault at **www.vault.com** for insider company profiles, expert advice, career message boards, expert resume reviews, the Vault Job Board and more.

VAULT CAREER LIBRARY   **127**

Uppers

There are many advantages to working as an independent contractor. I have a lot of freedom when it comes to arranging my schedule. Also, even though I'm working from home, I have the ability to communicate with a group of professionals doing what I do, many of whom work in other library jobs. It means having access to a broad range of experiences.

Downers

There are disadvantages too. Working as an independent contractor means that I am responsible for paying my own income tax, health insurance and retirement. Vacation means time off without pay. All of these are surmountable.

For me, the flexibility of the schedule and a professional hourly wage outweigh the other challenges. It's a good way to work, and to have a professional librarian position, without the rigidity of a routine schedule. I can grow my business as I choose by applying for other contract work. I can make it as big and challenging or as small and relaxed and I choose. It feels good to have control. And that's my daily life now.

Sharyl McMillian-Nelson

Genealogy Librarian

In a genealogy department, you deal with one specific question, and that question is, "I want to find out who my ancestors are. Where did they come from?" To answer this question, you need you start by handing the patron three crucial items: a pedigree chart/ancestor chart, a family group sheet and a good pencil. Then, a genealogy librarian will sit down with the patron, explaining to them what kinds of resources are available in the genealogy department. A short tour of the department may also be in order, so the patron can see how the department is organized. At my library, our books are not in Dewey Decimal system order; they are arranged alphabetically by state, then by county.

Types of research

There are various types of books available for patron use. The most common types found in a genealogy department are family histories written by the "family historian," state histories, county histories with family histories included, cemetery surveys and military histories. Due to the unique nature of some of the books, many libraries do not allow them to be loaned to other libraries.

Microfilm, filmed from original newspapers, consists of wills, deeds, marriage certificates, death certificates, voting registrations, censuses and military service records. Many genealogy departments will also have on microfilm the local newspaper, which can be used to obtain obituaries and articles about family members. Microfilm is also available through the Family History Library, associated with The Church of Jesus Christ of Latter-Day Saints, and The National Archives. A library's genealogical department can also counsel patrons on how to obtain microfilm from the above agencies.

Know your databases

These days, genealogy departments have another technological option available for their patrons—the electronic database. Among these, the preeminent is Ancestry.com, or for libraries, Ancestry.com Library Edition. This website consists of hundreds of databases in which a patron can search for everything from where Uncle Charlie lived in 1930 (by using the census), to what ship Aunt Louise came on when she came from England. A researcher could even get a picture of the ship if he wanted to. Through Ancestry World Tree, a patron can find other people around the world who are researching the same surname they are, or use a message board to try and find someone working on the same surname. Another important database used by genealogy departments is HeritageQuest.com. Though, not as extensive as Ancestry.com, it does contain the Periodical Source Index (PERSI), a comprehensive subject index found nowhere else and covering more than 6,300 genealogy and local history periodicals (only dating back to 1993 or so).

There are other numerous websites available for genealogical researchers, notably Cyndi's List of Genealogy Sites, a website put together by Cyndi Howells that lists thousands of genealogy websites from around the world.

So what do you need to be a genealogy librarian? A desire to learn, but also loads of patience, as well as the ability to listen. You will need patience to teach the patron how to use the materials and how to search a database, but you also have to be able to sit and listen to what they have to say.

Visit Vault at **www.vault.com** for insider company profiles, expert advice, career message boards, expert resume reviews, the Vault Job Board and more.

V/\ULT CAREER LIBRARY   **129**

Katherine Turton
Chattahoochee Valley Libraries
Columbus Public Library
Columbus, Georgia

Independent Information Professional

There is probably no such thing as a typical day as an info-entrepreneur, but here is what one of my days looked like recently.

After an early morning walk with the dogs, a quick breakfast and a scan of the morning paper, I commuted upstairs to my home office. I spent the first half-hour going through e-mail, and reading and contributing to the six or eight e-mail discussion lists I subscribe to. I replied to a query from a program planner who wanted to know my availability and rates to speak at a conference in six months, giving her a list of possible topics. I handled three subscription requests to my free monthly e-mail newsletters (www.BatesInfo.com/subscribe.html), and sent a pre-written reply to someone who asked about how to start an information business from home.

Then I settled down to the work of the day. I am in the middle of a project to identify the major buyers, manufacturers and uses of optical amplifiers, a job commissioned by a corporate librarian who just doesn't have the time to do it himself. I've already looked through websites of the major manufacturers, so I headed over to the professional online services to see what I can find in the industry press, technical journals and market research reports.

Document delivery

I noticed that two interesting articles aren't available in full text online; I sent an e-mail with the bibliographic citations to a document delivery company, which can arrange to have the articles photocopied, the royalties paid and the material e-mailed to me by the end of the day. I also noted several websites mentioned in the articles, finished off the rest of the web research for the job, created a table of the key players in the industry and wrote up an executive summary for the client. I put the project aside for later in the day— I like to let it percolate in my head for a few hours to make sure I didn't forget anything, and I have to wait for the articles to arrive from the doc del company.

Billing and invoicing

Since it was the end of the month, I sat down to do my monthly invoices and to pay my bills. I sent out reminder notices to two clients who are late in paying and a thank-you note to a new client. Just then, I got a call from a colleague, a public records researcher in California. She was digging up information on a scoundrel who, it seems, is bent on defrauding half of Florida. She wanted me to run an online search to see if he was mentioned in any Florida newspapers in the past five years. We settled on a not-to-exceed budget and deadline, and I thought to myself that my clients— Fortune 100 companies, corporate librarians, consultants and speechwriters, among others—often send me interesting work, but rarely do they ask me to track down real estate crooks.

After a short break to walk the dogs, I put in a couple of hours on a consulting project. A corporate librarian has been told that she needs to cut $700,000 from the information expenditures within her company, and she has asked me to review the company's current purchases. My job is to recommend ways to aggregate their information sources, eliminate duplication and fill any information gaps they may have.

Checking in with researchers

I glanced at the clock and realized that it is almost the end of the day on the East Coast, so I called a telephone researcher in Boston who is working on a phone project for one of my clients—getting standards for electrical power systems on ships—to check to see how the work is going. She told me that she would have a report for me, written up on my memo format and ready for me to send along to the client, by the end of the next day.

I will be traveling to Chicago next week to give a couple of talks on trends in the information industry. I had already sketched out my talks, and I opened up PowerPoint and polished up the talks.

I checked my e-mail and got a message from the document delivery company to whom I sent the request for the two articles on optical amplifiers. I looked over the articles, added a comment in the executive summary that I was sending to the client, inserted the articles in the report, saved the entire document in PDF and sent it on to the client.

Visit Vault at **www.vault.com** for insider company profiles, expert advice, career message boards, expert resume reviews, the Vault Job Board and more.

VAULT CAREER LIBRARY   **131**

Coaching

It was getting close to the end of the day, so I called a new independent info pro who I am coaching. We spent half an hour talking about her marketing strategy, how she was going to handle a difficult client situation and a seminar she is giving in a few months. By that time the dogs had started nudging my elbow—it was time for their evening walk, and they were getting impatient. I packed up some professional reading that I might or might not get to that evening, as another day at the global headquarters of Bates Information Services comes to a close.

Mary Ellen Bates
Owner of Bates Information Services

Children's Librarian: Public Library

Being a children's' librarian is an exciting, joyful, and demanding career. You have to be playful and energetic, but also professional; you have to enjoy the curiosity of young minds wanting to know everything about both you and the world around them. Singing and dancing to songs, and telling jokes, are indelible parts of my repertoire. Understanding both a child's wants and needs allows for a well-rounded relationship with the child and the community. And so besides being able to be playful, it is equally important that I be able to help a child with his or her homework assignments, that I know intimately the schools I cooperate with, and that I stay up-to-date with trends in popular young fiction. I am constantly ordering books for my children's collection, and I regularly attend community meetings in which I promote the library, its various programs and the supportive role the library can play in a child's development. I am an active member of several professional organizations and serve on committees within those organizations.

One of the activities I'm involved in is school visits, which entail classroom interaction either through stories or crafts. We also have a winter and summer reading club that I promote at schools and various youth organizations in my service area. Play-and-Learn, a weekly program, is an early literacy program for parents and their infants, and utilizes toys and board books in the learning process. I make math, vocabulary, or whatever worksheets are needed for those children struggling with a school subject. I find that most children want one-on-one time with me, whether I am reading to them, listening to them read or learning more about them. At the moment, I am planning a weekly crocheting get-together for adults and children.

Not just children

Being a children's librarian does not mean that I work only with children. From veterans interested in applying for benefits to patrons searching for rare books to people looking for family that have been lost to them, I am dedicated to helping whomever comes to the library to the best of my ability. Education is a fundamental service of any library; I have helped students of every age, whether they are learning addition and subtraction, pursuing their GED or doing research for their graduate studies. I like that I have the opportunity to meet so many different people and to become trusted friends to a great many of them. Their concerns and interests sometimes become my projects: my crocheting program developed out of a patron's desire to preserve that craft, a pastime of her grandmother's. Every day, I return to work knowing that I'll be exposed to new and exciting people and ideas. I simply couldn't ask for a more fulfilling career.

Diana DeVore
Librarian II – Cleveland Public Library, Cleveland, Ohio

Collection Development Librarian

As presented in library school, collection development is a fairly straightforward process. A lot of work, to be sure, and it was also clear that knowledge of a given subject area or genre was something that only came with time. Nevertheless, it was taken for granted that the process itself—locating vendors, buying books—would run rather smoothly.

When the co-worker responsible for collection development in foreign languages left for a new job, I was asked to take over. I already spoke and read Spanish (and some French) and had cataloged many of the library's Portuguese books, so I felt at home with the collection to a degree that many of my colleagues did not. I enjoy reading about other literatures and cultures, so I was looking forward to learning more about popular Brazilian novels or Francophone Caribbean nonfiction.

Dealing with municipal funds

What I did not expect was an education in how cumbersome the actual process of buying books using municipal government funds could sometimes be. When I first began as community languages librarian, we were six months into the fiscal year, which meant most community languages collection development money was already committed to specific vendors.

(In some municipal governments, departments that spend city money must commit fairly early in the fiscal year to buying goods and services from specific vendors. This is called "encumbering money.") But if a vendor should suddenly be unable to deliver, say, the Portuguese or French books you want, you are still pretty much stuck with them unless it's very early in the fiscal year. You can cancel an encumbrance. But then you have to encumber those funds with a new vendor. And you must have explicit permission from the city to spend money with that vendor during the current fiscal year. The process of getting that permission can take up to two months. That's two months during which no new books in a specific language are coming in, and two months that you simply cannot do part of your job.

Why wouldn't a vendor be able to deliver the books you want? And wouldn't you check what a vendor has in stock before committing to doing business with them? Some foreign language vendors have websites or catalogs listing extensive holdings. Under a given title it may say, "ready to ship now" or "available to ship in three weeks." In the case of some vendors, both statements may be a little optimistic. The biggest markets for foreign language books in this country are Spanish (specifically Mexican) and Chinese; they can support vendors with ample stock and adequate staff. A librarian interested in books from Brazil or Bangladesh is going to be dealing with new, small businesses that serve a much smaller market. They cannot afford the amply stocked warehouses (or numerous customer service staff) of Baker & Taylor or Ingram. They advertise books from overseas that they have every reason to believe they can provide. And it sometimes just doesn't happen.

The story of one vendor

In the case of one vendor of Portuguese language books from Brazil, my first experiences were wonderful. Based on circulation statistics from previous years and subject/genre gaps in our Portuguese collection, I browsed the online catalog by subject, picked out some titles and they arrived in a three weeks. I placed more orders, with the same result. Then I placed another order and nothing arrived. A month later I received a call from the vendor saying the books I had ordered were simply not available. He told me the Brazilian publishers said they could not send them. No reason given. Reviewing my order, I simply said, "Send me what you have in your warehouse in the areas of young adult fiction, murder mysteries (either originally written in Portuguese or in translation) and books on managing diabetes." The second year I did business with this vendor, he became increasingly unable to provide the specific titles advertised in his catalog. Soon he stopped answering phone calls. Soon after that his website was down. Lesson learned: Bookselling is a dicey business, and he was serving a very small market. Businesses sometimes fail.

I love my job. I love getting paid to know about new editions of the novels of Machado de Assis or to discover Mexican mystery writers. But vendors who disappear, vendors who can't fill orders, dealing with arcane purchasing procedures—that's the sort of thing you don't learn in library school—and that you'll find out on the job. You read it here first.

Kevin O'Kelly
Reference and Cataloging Librarian
Somerville Public Library.
Somerville, Mass.

Visit Vault at **www.vault.com** for insider company profiles, expert advice, career message boards, expert resume reviews, the Vault Job Board and more.

VAULT CAREER LIBRARY   135

FINAL ANALYSIS

Final Analysis

Many people stumble into careers with little research or planning. To avoid stumbling, go to a career counseling center at your college or elsewhere. This author has known a number of people who took a battery of tests and among the careers they were suited for was librarian. They didn't see themselves as librarians and took another path—only to return to the idea of a career in librarianship later after struggling on the career path they had chosen. This author was one of those people. Her mother tells her that as a child, she said she wanted to be a librarian when she grew up. Once in college, she changed her major four times and finally ended up getting a degree in business because she had the most credits in that area. When she thought about the courses she enjoyed the most, they were technology or research-related.

What are your interests, your values and your skills? There are many tests to help you assess, such as the Career Ability Placement Survey, the Career Assessment Inventory, the Myers-Briggs Type Indication and the Strong Interest Inventories. These tests can only identify options—you still need to do the hard work of self-examination.

Take a proactive approach. Talk to working librarians in different types of libraries. Ask them what they do, ask them what they like about their jobs, ask them why they became librarians. Peruse the many resources listed in this career guide. Go to your library and request copies of the books listed. Go to a couple of libraries and just hang out a couple of hours. Volunteer at a library. Get a student worker job at a library. Read blogs by librarians (The Shifted Librarian, Librarian.net and Librarian Avengers). Do your research. You may be rewarded with a stimulating and fulfilling career as a librarian.

As you consider your future in librarianship, here are some choice quotations about libraries and librarians.

"Perhaps no place in any community is so totally democratic as the town library. The only entrance requirement is interest." —Lady Bird Johnson.

"Librarians see themselves as the guardians of the First Amendment. You've got a thousand Mother Jones at the barricades! I love the librarians, and I am grateful for them! Librarians are one terrorist group you don't want to mess with." —Michael Moore.

"I'm of a fearsome mind to throw my arms around every living librarian who crosses my path, on behalf of the souls they never knew they saved." — Barbara Kingsolver

"I have always imagined that Paradise will be a kind of library." — Jorge Luis Borges

"Information is the currency of democracy." —Thomas Jefferson

"Throughout my formal education I spent many, many hours in public and school libraries. Libraries became courts of last resort, as it were. The current definitive answer to almost any question can be found within the four walls of most libraries." —Arthur Ashe

"Whatever the cost of our libraries, the price is cheap compared to that of an ignorant nation." —Walter Cronkite

APPENDIX

Helpful Resources

Associations and Organizations

American Association of Law Librarians

www.aallnet.org/

American Association of School Librarians (AASL)

ala.org/ala/mgrps/divs/aasl/index.cfm

American Library Association (ALA)

www.ala.org/

American Society for Information and Technology

www.asis.org

American Theological Librarians Association

www.atla.com/atlahome.html

Association of College and Research Libraries

www.ala.org/ala/mgrps/divs/acrl/index.cfm

Association for Record Managers and Administrators

www.arma.org/

Art Libraries Association of North America http:

www.arlisna.org/

Catholic Library Association

www.cathla.org/

The Independent Information Professional

www.aiip.org/

International Federation of Library Associations and Institutions

www.ifla.org/

Library & Information Technology Association

www.ala.org/ala/mgrps/divs/lita/litahome.cfm

Medical Library Association (MLA)

www.mlanet.org/

Music Library Association

www.musiclibraryassoc.org/

Public Library Association (PLA)

www.ala.org/ala/mgrps/divs/pla/index.cfm

Society of American Archivists

www.archivists.org/

Society of Competitive Intelligence Professionals

www.scip.org/

Special Library Association (SLA)

www.sla.org/

Young Adult Library Services Association

www.ala.org/ala/mgrps/divs/yalsa/yalsa.cfm

Online Resources

Become a Librarian

http://www.becomealibrarian.org/

Blogs
iLibrarian

oedb.org/blogs/ilibrarian/

The Shifted Librarian

theshiftedlibrarian.com/

Library Avengers

librarianavengers.org/

Information Wants to be Free

meredith.wolfwater.com/wordpress/index.php

Tame the Web: Libraries, Technology and People

tametheweb.com/

Librarian.net–Putting the 'rarin back in Librarian since 1999

www.librarian.net/

Job Sources

The sources below list jobs for general and special types of libraries. Some of these sources allow you to post a resume, search by a geographic region or state, set up a RSS feed to receive new job announcements daily and some offer career guidance and articles related to the job search.

The big ones

ALA job list

joblist.ala.org/

ALA job list works like many of the major employment websites and offers searchable job postings as well as features such as the ability to post your resume for prospective employers or placement services.

LIBjobs

www.libjobs.com/

Combined job postings www.lisjobs.com/jobs/index.asp

New vacancies are posted daily.

Library & Information Technology Association Job list

www.ala.org/ala/mgrps/divs/lita/litaresources/litajobsite/litajobsite.cfm offers job searches by geographical region. New vacancies are posted each week on Wednesday morning.

Library job postings on the Internet

Visit Vault at **www.vault.com** for insider company profiles, expert advice, career message boards, expert resume reviews, the Vault Job Board and more.

VAULT CAREER LIBRARY   145

www.libraryjobpostings.org/

LISjobs

www.lisjobs.com also has a blog where career advice is discussed.

The others

American Association of Law Libraries Job Hotline

www.aallnet.org/hotline/hotline.asp

Art Libraries Society of North America

www.arlisna.org/jobnet.html

Asian Pacific American Librarians Association

www.apalaweb.org/jobs/apalajobs.

Association of Research Libraries Career Resources

careers.arl.org/

Association Society for Information Science & Technology

www.jobtarget.com/home/index.cfm?site_id=180

The Chronicle of Higher Education Chronicle Careers

chronicle.com/jobs/

Library of Congress Job Opportunities

www.loc.gov/hr/employment/index.php

Major Orchestra Librarians' Association

www.mola-inc.org/

Medical Library Association Jobs

www.mlanet.org/jobs/jobs.html

Music Library Association Job Openings

www.musiclibraryassoc.org/employmentanded/joblist/openings.shtml

News Library Jobs

www.ibiblio.org/slanews/jobs/jobs.html

SCIP (Society of Competitive Intelligence Professionals)

www.jobtarget.com/c/search_results.cfm?site_id=

Special Library Association

careercenter.sla.org/search/browse/

Staffing agencies and consultants

Cadence Group

www.cadence-group.com/jobs.htm

C. Berger Groups

www.cberger.com/

Heller and Associates

www.hellerandassociates.com/

InfoCurrent

www.infocurrent.com/

Infotrieve

www4.infotrieve.com/careers/search_jobs.asp

Keister and Associates

www.johnkeister.com/

Labat-Anderson Incorporated

www.labat.com/jobs.htm

Library Associates Companies

www.libraryassociates.com/

LSSI

www.lssi.com/openjobs.cfm

International opportunities

Jobs in the U.K.

ASLIB-Professional Recruitment Ltd.

Visit Vault at **www.vault.com** for insider company profiles, expert advice, career message boards, expert resume reviews, the Vault Job Board and more.

V/\ULT CAREER LIBRARY   **147**

www.aslib.com/recruitment/sys/jobs_main.php

Infotrieve

www. corporate.infotrieve.com/careers

TFPL–The Information People

www.tfpl.com/

Peace Corps

www.peacecorps.gov/index.cfm?shell=pchq.jobs

Positions in Canada

The Partnership Job Board

www.libraryjobs.ca/page/find%20jobs/ezlist_posts.aspx

Positions in Australia

Australian Library and Information Association

www.alia.org.au/employment/vacancies/

Positions in New Zealand

LIANZA

www.lianza.org.nz/development/employers/index.html

Recommended Reading

Accidental Librarian. Pamela H. Mackellar. 2008. Information Today, Inc.

A Day in the Life: Career Options in Library and Information Science. By Priscilla Schontz and Richard Murray, 2007, Libraries Unlimited, Inc.

Casanova Was a Librarian: A Light-Hearted Look at the Profession. By Katherine Low. McFarland and Company.

Free For All: Oddballs, Geeks, and Gangstas in the Public Library. By Dan Borchert, 2007, Virgin Books.

Library. By Stephen Akey. 2002, Orchises Press.

The NextGen Librarian's Survival Guide. By Rachel Singer Gordon, 2006, Information Today, Inc.

Quiet Please: Dispatches from a Public Librarian. By Scott Douglas. 2008, De Capo Press.

Rethinking Information Work: A Career Guide for Librarians and Other Information Professionals. by G. Kim Dority, 2006, Libraries Unlimited Inc.

What's the Alternative? Career Option for Librarians and Info Pros. By Rachel Singer Gordon, 2008, Information Today, Inc.

Visit Vault at **www.vault.com** for insider company profiles, expert advice, career message boards, expert resume reviews, the Vault Job Board and more.

V/ULT CAREER LIBRARY   149

About the Author

Deborah (Deb) A. Sommer received her MSLS from the University of Tennessee-Knoxville. She has worked as a librarian at the University of North Carolina-Wilmington, the University of Georgia, Vanderbilt University and the University of Missouri as the Regional Librarian for the National Network of Medical Libraries. Sommer established the first nationwide Small Business Information Service funded by the U.S. Small Business Administration. Sommer has been an administrative librarian with the U.S. Forest Service, and director of the Walker Management Library at Vanderbilt University. She has also freelanced as a virtual reference librarian with OCLC. She is currently the Director of the Metropolis Public Library in Metropolis, Illinois.

Visit the Vault Finance Career Channel at **www.vault.com/finance**–with
insider firm profiles, message boards, the Vault Finance Job Board and more.

VAULT CAREER LIBRARY   151